# Contents

# INTRODUCTION

Information technology influences all our lives. So many everyday things are controlled, to some extent, by computers: borrowing a library book, going shopping, withdrawing money from the bank, setting a video, using a microwave or the washing machine. Most of us manage these everyday events easily and without a second thought.

The use of information technology is growing all the time both in the extent to which it is used and the speed with which a variety of operations can be undertaken. Our children need to become familiar with this technology not so much in how it works but how it can help and support their learning.

Computers are commonplace in schools, and this book suggests way of introducing information technology and using this technology across the curriculum. Some of the activities are intended to increase the children's understanding of the technology itself, but most are intended to support curriculum activities in a way that enhances learning and extends the range of work the children can undertake.

Our main message is that the use of IT can stimulate and motivate children in all areas of the curriculum, and above all it can be fun for the children and the teacher.

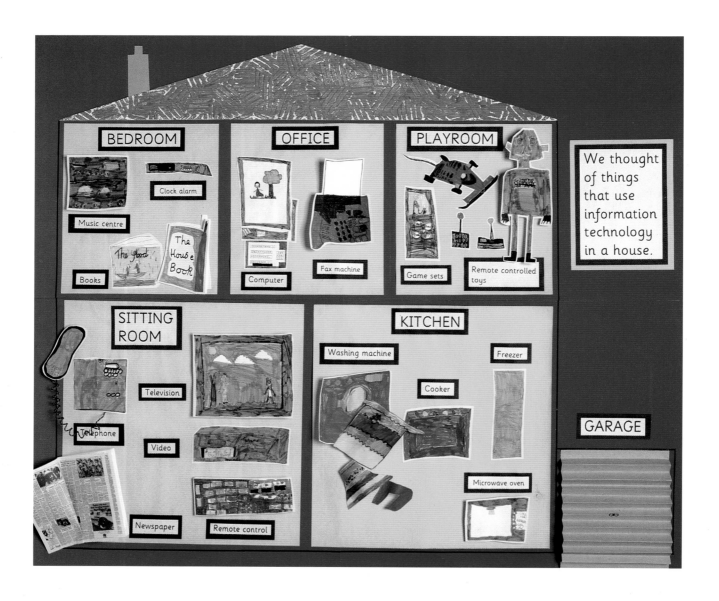

# THE USE OF INFORMATION TECHNOLOGY IN EVERYDAY LIFE

Ask the children if they can think of ways in which we use computers. (Remind them that computers are machines that can do things with information.)

The children will probably talk about personal computers at home or in the classroom, and computer games.

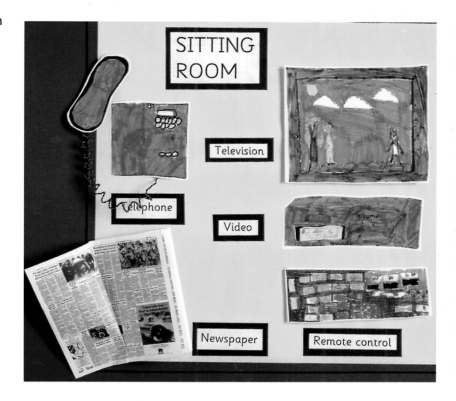

## INFORMATION TECHNOLOGY IN SCHOOL

- Take the children on a walk around the school and ask them to see if they can identify anything that uses a computer to make it work. Encourage the children to make their own suggestions but draw their attention to the following things:

| | |
|---|---|
| **television and videos** - | Chips in the television receive the signals and text data, store pictures and operate the remote control |
| **books** - | Most books are written and designed using desk top publishing |
| **burglar alarms** - | The control box uses computer technology. The sensors detect movement |
| **electronic keyboards** - | Electrical signals are changed into sound waves |
| **calculators** - | Number information is stored and manipulated. |

- Focus on the use of information technology in the school office. If possible, arrange a time with the school secretary when the children can visit the office. Show the children the office equipment that uses information technology:

| | |
|---|---|
| **telephone** - | Computers connect the calls. Numbers are stored in the computer memory |
| **answerphones** - | Messages are recorded electronically |
| **fax machines** - | Send messages via telephone lines. They translate the text into electronic code |
| **computers** - | Store information and word process. |

- Demonstrate how the equipment is used.

- If the school office has a fax machine, use it with the children to send a message. If you have contacts with a colleague in another school, arrange for a transfer of messages between two classes. Talk to the children about the kind of good wishes they can send - let the children draw or write their message on the 'class' paper. With careful co-ordination the children will be able to watch the sending and receipt of the messages.

---

**FAX MESSAGE**

**To:** Our friends at Whitefields School
**From:** Class 2, Giles Street School
**Date:** Monday, 12th September
**Message**:

We hope that you had a good holiday. We are looking forward to the new term.

---

# OTHER APPLICATIONS OF INFORMATION TECHNOLOGY

Choose some specific applications to focus on, for example:

## THE POSTAL SYSTEM

• Collect used envelopes for the children to look at. Draw their attention to the postcode. Talk to the children about how letters are delivered - describing the sequence from the time that the letter is written to its delivery. Explain that when the letter reaches the sorting office the envelope is scanned and the postcode (or zip code) is turned into magnetic ink which the computer can 'read'. This allows the computer to tell where the letter is going very quickly.

• Tell the children the postcode of the school. Ask them to find out their postcode at home and the postcode of friends and relations further afield.

• When the class has gathered a collection of different postcodes, look at them closely to see if the children can detect any patterns - for example, that their postcodes are likely to be very similar, that the first letters will be part of the name of a big town close to their homes. Use a map to show the children where the locations of different postcodes are.

• Let the children choose an address of a distant friend or relative to write on a decorated envelope. **Display the envelopes around a map of the country with coloured strings indicating the destination of the letter.**

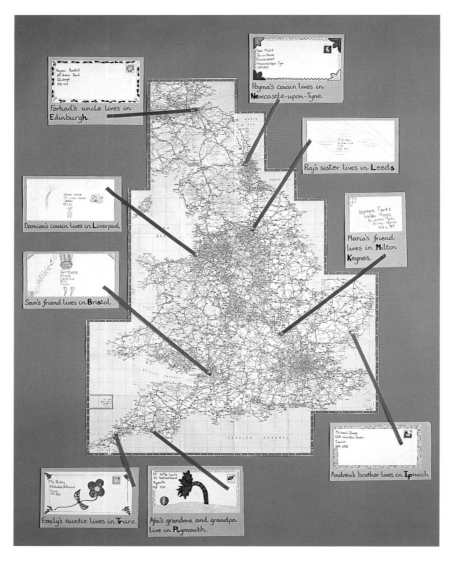

## SMART CARDS

Everyone has more and more cards which use technology to store and transmit information. Show the children a variety - bank cards, credit or store cards, library cards, membership cards, etc. Encourage the children to identify the cards, describe their function and how they are used.

- Show the children the magnetic strip on the back of a card which is where the information is stored. Relate this to a bank card. Tell the children how someone has to tap in a personal number which the computer compares with the information on the strip.

## SHOPPING

- Collect packaging from a variety of objects. Draw the children's attention to the bar codes on the packages. Encourage the children to notice details in the code - the different width of the stripes, the numbers - and that different products have different codes. Ask the children how shop assistants in the larger stores use the bar codes.

- Let the children look around the classroom to see if they can find any other things which have bar codes on.

- Explain how the bar codes work, and that each product has its own particular code. When the assistant passes the code over a laser, the code is 'read', the black and white pattern is changed into electronic signals. This allows the shop to know how many items are sold, and also records the price.

- Establish a shop in an area of the classroom. Incorporate aspects of information technology in the area - a 'pretend' scanner, a calculator and print-outs of the stock in the shop.

- Extend the work on bar codes into an exploration of black and white patterns. Talk to the children about the stripes on the code: introduce the word 'column'. Ask them to think of other words to describe patterns - spotted, diamonds, check, etc.

- Provide the children with a range of materials: for example, felt-tip pens, pencils, paints, charcoal, wax crayons (all in black), and ask them to create their own black and white pattern. Display the children's work.

## ROBOTS

- Introduce this work by explaining that robots are machines, frequently controlled by information technology, which can do certain tasks.

- Gather together relevant reference books and ask the children to use these books to find out what robots are used for. Write down all the activities that the children find. Explain that robots are often used for tasks that are either very repetitive, require great precision or are dangerous. Let the children look at the list that they have compiled and sort out the jobs into the three categories.

  Encourage the children to reflect on why robots are more suitable for these activities than people would be.

| Repetitive jobs | Precision jobs | Dangerous jobs |
| --- | --- | --- |
| Working in a factory<br>Milking cows | Automatic pilot<br>Surgery<br>Cutting jewels | Underwater exploration<br>Bomb disposal |

- Many constructional kits will allow the children to explore features associated with robots - extending mechanical arms, roller wheels, clasping grips, etc.

- Use an activity which uses robots to reinforce the children's sequencing skills. A manufacturing task is probably one of the most suitable: for example, a car factory. Talk to the children about the sequence of activities that take place. Divide the class into small groups and assign one element of the car manufacturing process to each group.

  When the groups have finished drawing their picture, let the children sort the pictures into the correct order. Use reference books to support this work.

- Discuss with the children what they would like a robot to do. Talk to them about what features the robot would have to have to enable it to complete the task, and then ask them to draw their robot. Provide the children with a range of junk modelling materials to make their robot, using their drawing as a design brief.

- **Let the children name their robot and write about how they would use it (see photograph on facing page).**

- Use robots as a stimulus for imaginative writing.

- There are many children's books that have robots as characters. Make a display of these books in the classroom.

- Draw on the children's knowledge of robots in popular culture (the Daleks from 'Dr Who', C3PO and R2D2 from 'Star Wars') to fire their imagination. Endeavour to play down any associated violence.

- Create a class story about a robot. Start the story off with a sentence about a robot: for example, 'A long time ago I had a marvellous robot, but one day it all went terribly wrong...'. The children then take it in turns to say the next sentence of the story. Use a tape recorder to record the story. Transcribe the story and make it into a big class book. Let the children illustrate the story.

  Make the tape and the book readily accessible for the children to look and listen to.

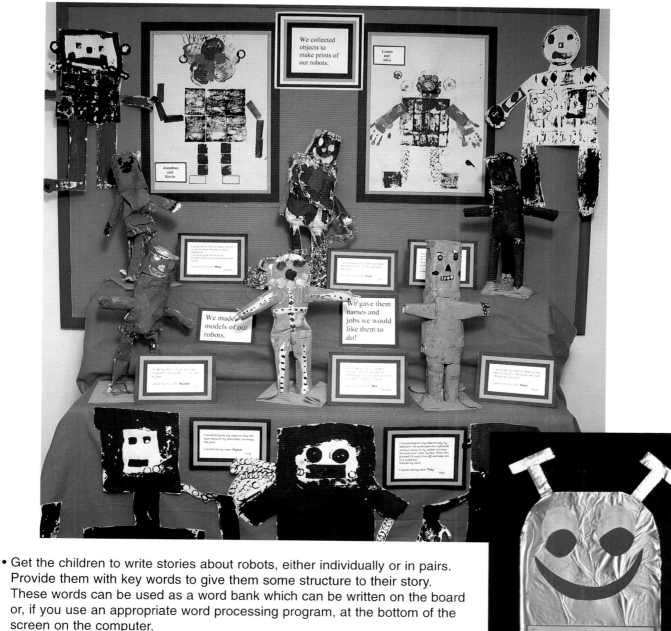

- Get the children to write stories about robots, either individually or in pairs. Provide them with key words to give them some structure to their story. These words can be used as a word bank which can be written on the board or, if you use an appropriate word processing program, at the bottom of the screen on the computer.

- Display the children's stories or make them into a class collection. Make the class book more interesting by cutting the book into a robot shape.

- Robot stories are very suitable for recording in a cartoon form.

- Get the children to make two-dimensional models of the robots in their stories. Tell them to draw their robot and then to identify the major parts of their robot. They then draw the individual parts and join these using butterfly clips. This will allow the robots to move in a disjointed, mechanical way.

- Display these with the children's writing.

# INTRODUCING INFORMATION TECHNOLOGY

Most children will be aware of computers when they start school and so it is appropriate to introduce information technology by investigating computers.

- Explain to the children that a computer is a machine. It takes in information (data), it follows what people tell it to do with the data, it can produce the results and it can store information.

- Compare a computer with a human brain. Encourage the children to think of similarities and differences. Let one group of children paint a large picture of a person and another group a picture of a computer. Brainstorm with the children what computers and people can do. Write down their ideas and display them by the pictures.

- Ensure that the children can see a computer when you introduce the children to the parts of a computer. Find out if the children know the names of the main parts - keyboard, monitor, printer and the computer box containing the hard disc. (Explain that the hard disc is where all the information is kept.) The depth of explanation will depend on the children's previous experience and abilities.

| What people can do | What computers can do |
|---|---|
| * use information | * use information |
| * keep things in their memory | * keep things in their memory |
| * work | * work very quickly |
| * feel things | |

- Introduce new vocabulary - mouse, floppy disc, cursor, pointer. Explain why a mouse is so called (because of its shape, and the lead resembling a tail), and how the floppy discs are protected by a hard plastic cover.

- Assign different parts of the computer for the children to draw and paint. Label the relevant parts.

## KEYBOARDS

Traditional keyboards are organised using the QWERTY format. It is possible to buy keyboards arranged in alphabetical order but, as the children are bound to meet the QWERTY format at some stage, it seems better to familiarise them with it as soon as possible

- Keyboards use capital letters and the children may well be more familiar with lower case letters. Use this as opportunity to reinforce children's knowledge of lower case and capital letters.

• Draw a model of the QWERTY keyboard. Leave a space on each key for the children to write the lower case letter. Children can keep these to refer to when using the keyboards.

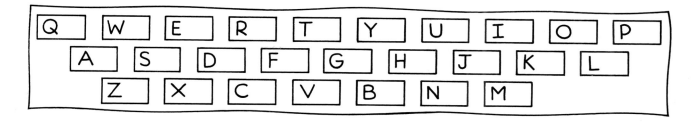

• Make an alphabet frieze with the children. Each child is given a letter to draw and decorate, in its capital and lower case form. When all the children have finished, work with the group to sort the letters into correct order.

Display the frieze near the computer.

    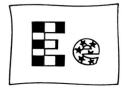

## ICONS
Many software programs use icons.

• Tell the children that icons are small pictures which indicate the various functions of the computer.

• Show the children examples of icons on different programs.

• Ask the children to design their own icons.

• Expand the discussion by talking about other symbols in everyday life: social sign symbols (for toilets, etc.), symbols on food packaging and road signs. Create a display of all the examples that the children find.

## LEARNING COMPUTER COMMANDS

As the children become more familiar with the computer they will be introduced to certain commands which are common to most programs. The most important are:

**save, print, quit/exit, edit, cut, copy, paste.**

The order and speed at which you introduce them will depend on the children's developing competence.

• When introducing a command, check that the children understand the meaning of the word in a non-technological sense. For example, if introducing *quit* or *exit*, ask the children if they can think where they might have seen the word *exit* (for example, in a cinema).

• Saving their work is one of the most, if not the most, important skills. Talk to the children about the kind of things that they save at home - they are usually things that are precious or important to them.

Make a wall display of all the things that the children consider precious and would wish to keep safe.

• Emphasise that they need to know how to save their work because it is important. Go through the sequence of commands that you have to follow to save work. Let the children write or draw the sequence. Let the children demonstrate to you how they save their work.

• Make a simple record book or sheet which will allow the children to record their own achievements with information technology.

The booklets can be made more interesting by making them computer shaped.

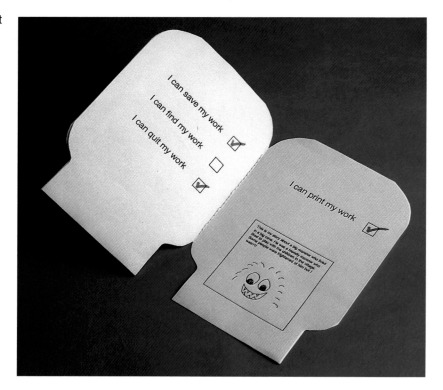

12

# SETTING UP A COMPUTER AREA
# IN THE CLASSROOM

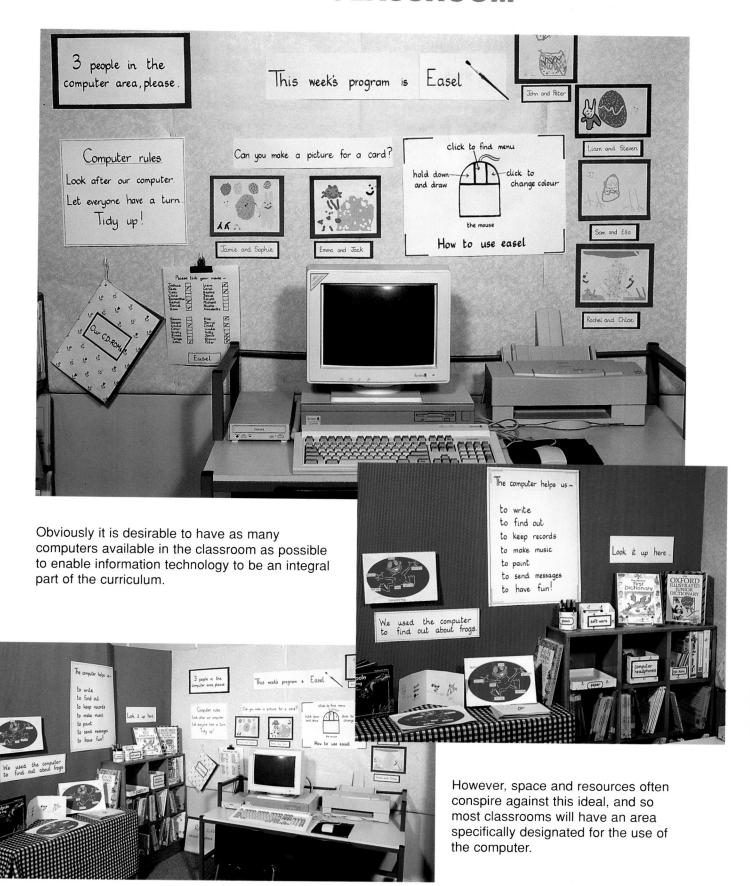

Obviously it is desirable to have as many computers available in the classroom as possible to enable information technology to be an integral part of the curriculum.

However, space and resources often conspire against this ideal, and so most classrooms will have an area specifically designated for the use of the computer.

When organising this area it is important to consider certain things.

- The computer should be positioned so that a direct light source does not fall on the screen (making it difficult to see).

- The chairs should be at the correct height to ensure that the children sit with a correct posture.

- Make sure that wires are tucked away and do not create a health and safety problem.

- There should be sufficient room on the table for the children to use it as a work station, bringing all their required work things with them to the computer. There should be plenty of room for additional information technology features: for example, concept keyboards.

- Organise the necessary support equipment carefully. Keep a catalogue of any CD-ROMs that you have. This catalogue should be readily accessible to the children.

- Use folders for keeping concept keyboard overlays. Keep a catalogue of these for easy access.

- As the children become familiar with specific programs or CD-ROMs, let them describe what the programs can do. Ask the children to write this down and display their writing in the computer area.

- Emphasise that computers are a support for learning by making the computer area a general reference area. Use bookshelves to display general reference and information texts.

- As with other areas in the classroom, it is important to establish a code of conduct or set of rules which the children must follow when using the computer. Rules are always more effective if they have been negotiated with the children. Tell the children that they need rules that will make sure they are safe, and other rules which will make sure that everyone has a fair share of time on the computers. When you and the children have generated an appropriate list of rules, write them on a piece of card which the children could illustrate. Display the rules in a prominent place in the computer area.

Remember rules should always be expressed positively.

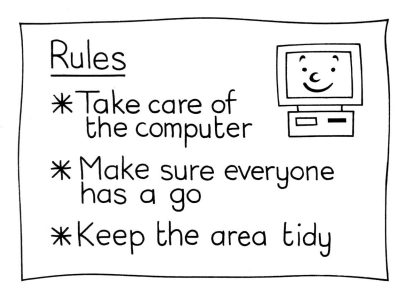

- The computer will be used for a variety of reasons - you will be using it to teach children specific aspects related to information technology: it will be used to support learning (for example, children will be writing and drafting using word processing, using it to organise data, using programs which reinforce a range of concepts, etc.); it will be used as an art resource; CD-ROMs will be a reference source, and it can also be a recreational activity. Display work in the computer area which reflects as many of these facilities as possible.

• To emphasise the importance of computers in everyday life, integrate a computer into an imaginative play area, from time to time.

A bank: incorporate tellers' windows and a manager's desk. Get the children to make an automatic cash dispenser using a large cardboard box. Let the children use the computer for writing letters to customers and for checking the amount of money in accounts.

A shop: the computer can be used for writing posters for the shop displays and for checking the stock. Accounts will be kept by computer.

A library: the computer is used for keeping details about the borrowers, for recording the books borrowed, etc.

A hospital: the computer will hold patients' details, keeping a stock of the medicines, writing appointment letters, etc.

Other possible play areas which would include a computer - a post office, a theatre and a school.

SCREEN SAVERS

Screen savers are used to prevent a static image 'burning' into the screen. They can provide an excellent stimulus for artwork. Many of the screen savers that are available are very inventive. Show the children examples of existing screen savers. Ask the children to study them closely and to identify anything that they feel they have in common: for example, that they all move. This will allow you to explain the purpose of the screen saver.

Design a screen saver with the children.

As the screen savers involve movement, show the children how to create a story board which will show how the screen changes over time.

## • Geometric patterns

Many of the screen savers are based on changing geometric patterns: these resemble kaleidoscopes. If you have a kaleidoscope in the classroom let the children look at it, encouraging them to observe closely how the shapes and colours change as the kaleidoscope is moved. Provide the children with five pieces of paper and ask them to draw their screen saver as it changes its sequence.

 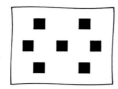 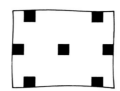 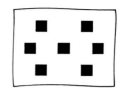 

## • Screen saver 'stories'

These stories may have a traditional narrative line or may show something like a change in nature; for example, a tadpole changing into a frog, a flower opening, etc. Use books and photographs (particularly the slow frame exposure of changes) to develop the children's ideas. Emphasise to the children that the screens are frequently highly coloured.

We designed story boards to make a screen saver for the computer.

Screen Savers

Display the children's story boards or one exemplar screen.

# COMPUTER APPLICATIONS

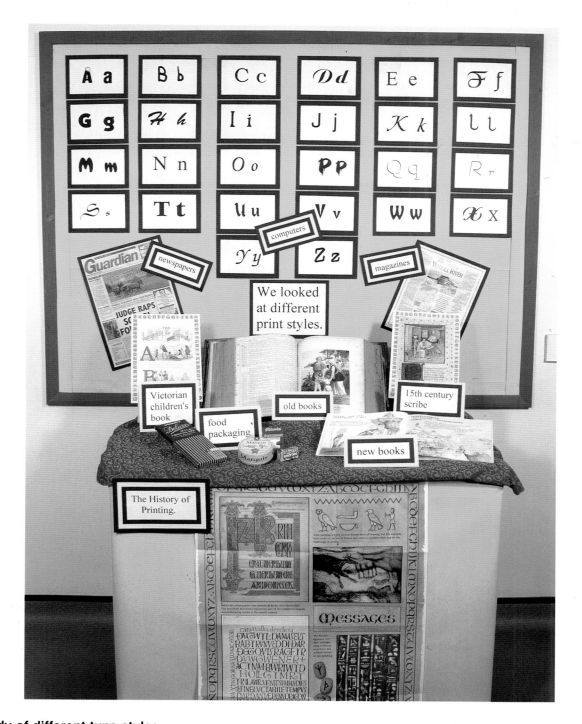

**A study of different type styles**

## WORD PROCESSING

Word processing applications are perhaps the most useful and the most used of the applications for a computer. There are many on the market, several of which are simplified for use with children. If you have a computer with a speech facility the children will be able to hear what they type.

Some applications have the facility to display common words or a topic vocabulary at the bottom of the screen. These can be added by the teacher and are worth seeking out.

To introduce the children to word processing, start by collecting together books on printing, the alphabet, manuscripts, etc. Discuss with the children the idea of printing in its historical context. Try to have some examples of hieroglyphics, different alphabets, for example, Japanese, Chinese, Cyrillic, etc.

Ask each child to copy or invent a different print style, either from a historical source or from a current source, for example, advertising, magazines, newspapers, street signs, etc. Some of the children could undertake potato cuts, using half a potato for each letter. Lino cuts are also a good way of demonstrating the printing process.

Make a large classroom display of different type styles **(see photographs on previous page, and below).**

The children need to become familiar with upper and lower case letters, especially to use the keyboard which has upper case. Ask each child to draw a particular lower and upper case letter of the alphabet. These can be displayed in the classroom near to the computer area. Ask each pupil to make their own alphabet, both upper and lower case to keep for reference.

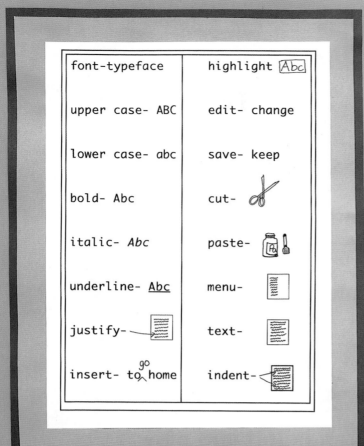

| font-typeface | highlight Abc |
|---|---|
| upper case- ABC | edit- change |
| lower case- abc | save- keep |
| bold- Abc | cut- ✂ |
| italic- *Abc* | paste- |
| underline- <u>Abc</u> | menu- |
| justify- | text- |
| insert- to<sup>go</sup>home | indent- |

Introduce the children to the language of word processing.

Make a wall display of words with their meanings using either pictures or words. The teacher could print off the words and the children supply the illustrations.

It is unlikely that the children will need to use many of these commands on a regular basis, but it is important that they become familiar with the terms and have a ready reference to look at.

To accustom the children to the use of, and the basic functions of, the computer, ask each child to print their own names either in upper or lower case on the computer.

Once the children have typed their names, show them how they may:

- change the size of the print
- underline their name
- change the print to italic print
- make the print bold
- change the font (typeface).

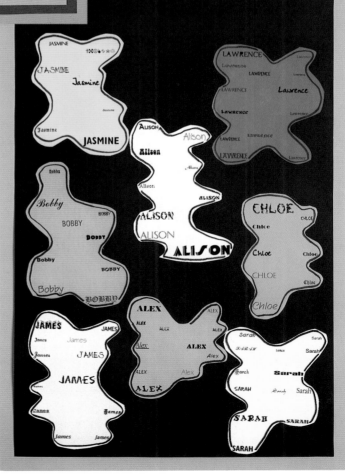

To introduce the children to one of the most valuable functions of a word processing application - that is, the ease with which text can be moved around, it is a good idea to undertake the task on paper first.

Tell the children a short, well-known fairy tale or nursery rhyme, for example, 'Mary had a little lamb'. Divide the children into groups of four. Ask each child to write one line of the rhyme on a strip of paper.

| **And everywhere that Mary went** |
| --- |

| **Its fleece was white as snow** |
| --- |

| **That lamb was sure to go** |
| --- |

| **Mary had a little lamb** |
| --- |

| **It made the children laugh and play** |
| --- |

| **It followed her to school one day** |
| --- |

| **To see a lamb at school** |
| --- |

| **That was against the rule** |
| --- |

Ask the children to sort the lines of the story or rhyme into the correct order. They could number them first. Ask them to write the story/rhyme in the correct order.

Explain to the children that they can sort and change the order of their writing on the computer without having to write it out several times before they get it right. Allow each group to have an opportunity to do this using the 'cut and paste' facility - initially they could copy rhymes from a book.

Print the incorrect order and the correct order each time. The ones in the correct order can be used for sequencing activities with other groups of children.

> Mary had a little lamb
> Its fleece was white as snow
> And everywhere that Mary went
> That lamb was sure to go.
>
> It followed her to school one day
> That was against the rule
> It made the children laugh and play
> To see a lamb at school.

In order to give the children lots of practice using a word processing program, and to help them become familiar with the keyboard, many classroom labels can be made. Ask the children to think of all the possible labels needed both in the classroom and around the school. Hold a brainstorming session with them to get lots of ideas.

On the blackboard or a large piece of paper, record their ideas initially for the types of notices and labels required, for example, for storage items, for directions, for information, for naming, descriptions for display work, for instructions, etc.

Under each heading decide the labels or notices needed.

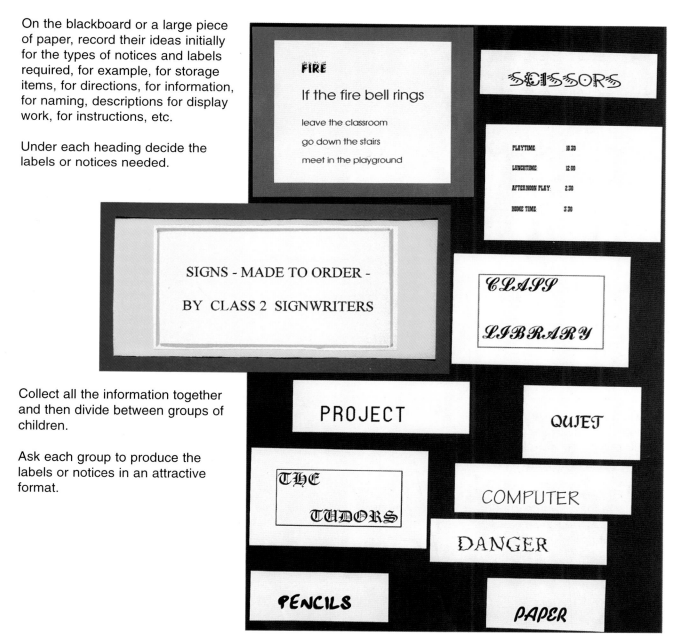

Collect all the information together and then divide between groups of children.

Ask each group to produce the labels or notices in an attractive format.

## Writing stories

A word processing application is ideal for developing children's story writing ability. It can be an opportunity to undertake more in-depth planning, drafting and re-drafting.

Children need to have a clear idea of 'story' if they are to be successful writers themselves. To achieve this, children need to listen to many stories of different genres and follow this with class discussion about how the story has been constructed and how the author has achieved certain aspects or effects within the story.

To start a story writing session, introduce a topic for the children to discuss after they have listened to several stories within the same genre, for example, adventure stories about dragons. Allow children to work at the computer in groups while writing a basic outline of their story. This would provide the beginning, the middle, the end and the main events. Print this off ready for the next stage.

Using the basic outline, ask the children to generate lists of words that they may need for their story. Print off the list ready for the next stage (see first section of photograph below).

Using this list can be an opportunity to work on basic grammatical structures. Ask the group to consider their word list and sort them into nouns, adjectives and verbs. Spellings can be corrected at this stage, and the new list printed off (see second section of photograph below).

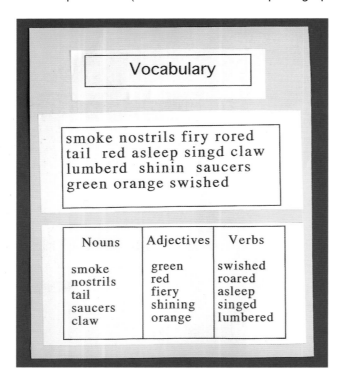

**List of vocabulary - before spelling is corrected**

**First draft – before spelling is corrected**

The group should now work on their first draft - on the computer - trying to combine the outline of the story and the word lists to produce an interesting and exciting story.

The group may want to print out their ideas several times until they are happy with the story.

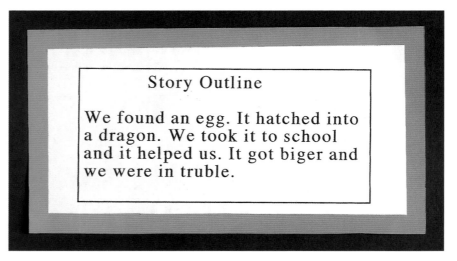

22

The next stage is essentially secretarial. The children should check their spelling, using the spell checker on the computer, if available. If not, the teacher could note any incorrrect spellings and ask the cihldren to look them up in a dictionary. They should check for capital letters, full stops, speech marks, etc. They should consider the layout of their work. They may wish to change the font or the spacing, to have both margins justified, etc.

**Second draft - before spelling and punctuation are corrected**

> ### Second Draft
>
> On the way home we found an egg in the ditch. We took it home and it hatched into a tiny dragon. it was green. we put it in a box and took it to school. our techer didnt know but it got bigger and bigger. The dragon could talk and it did our sums. it had fiery breath and eyes like saucers its claws were long and pointed. it had wings and it flew away.

Once the children are happy with their work, the story can be printed. The work could be published in a class book or mounted for a wall display.

The children could use the painting program to produce illustrations for their work, or paint them in the usual way.

A DRAGON'S TALE

On the way home yesterday we found an egg in a ditch. We took it home and put it in a warm cupboard. In the morning it had hatched into a tiny dragon. It was green with tiny nostrils that smoked. We put it in a box and took it to school. We didn't tell our teacher. It got bigger and bigger. It could talk and it did our sums. We got them all right and we got a star. All the time it grew and grew. It started to have fiery breathand its eyes were like saucers. Its claws were long and shiny. Its teeth were pointed. We started to get very scared of the dragon and we thought our teacher would be cross. Gemma had a brilliant idea. She got some cheese from the kitchen and let the dragon follow her down to the pond. She threw the cheese in the pond and the dragon jumped in to get it. He couldn't swim so he drowned.

**Publishing a newspaper**

Many computer applications can be combined in the publishing of a class newspaper - word processing, drawing and painting. It also combines a number of skills: writing, editing, drawing, designing, etc., and provides a sense of audience for the children. Most word processing applications can be used for desk top publishing using the various formatting commands.

A visit to a local newspaper office would be a good introduction - or a local journalist or editor could be asked to come and talk to the children. This could be followed by examining newspapers in class. It is better to study a local paper rather than a national newspaper, as it will be more relevant to the way the children will proceed in class.

Ask the children to look at the newspapers, and draw their attention to the following:

| | |
|---|---|
| **overall design** | **use of headlines** |
| **pictures/photographs** | **headings** |
| **types of articles** | **information published** |
| **advertisements** | **regular features** |

Discuss with the children the sort of information, news, stories, articles, etc., that they would be able to publish in a class newspaper. Start to list these on a large sheet of paper.

The children need to become familiar with certain techniques and skills before proceeding too far with any writing.

- If they plan to interview others, will they use a tape recorder or make written notes? Can they use the tape recorder easily? Will they need to write a questionnaire before they start?

- If they plan to take photographs, are they familiar with the camera? It is possible to have a roll of film printed on to a CD-ROM disk which can be loaded into the computer. You may have a digital camera available that will transfer photographs directly into the computer for publishing. (There are also scanners that allow a picture or text to be scanned into the computer.)

- **There may be some clip art on the computer that could be used in the newspaper.** Allow the children to look at what is available. It is also worth printing out a list of all the fonts that are available so the children can make a choice and think carefully about design issues.

All or any of these will make the project interesting for the children and should be considered before the work begins.

Using the list previously generated, make a final decision about the articles, information, etc., that the children will work on.

It is worth considering the timing of publishing a newspaper. It may be possible to devote a large part of one whole week to the work. This would provide a more genuine feel to the work and deadlines can be set in a realistic way. If it is drawn out over several weeks the immediacy can be lost. It would also be difficult to work on genuine news over a period of weeks.

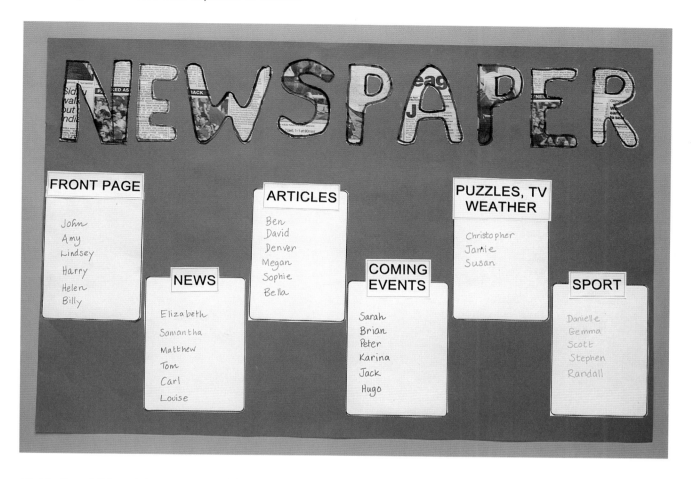

Divide the children into groups, making each group responsible for a page. Each group should work on a different aspect of the paper. At the end of each day hold a meeting for all the teams so they can describe the work they have covered so far, and consider if any changes need to be made. It is important that children begin to develop the ability to reflect on their own work, offer and accept constructive criticism and adjust their plans to fit in with the overall planning.

Make a large notice that will provide the following information:

- Group membership

- Topic for each group - leave sufficient space for the children to write their individual jobs once they have been decided

- The overall plan for the week.

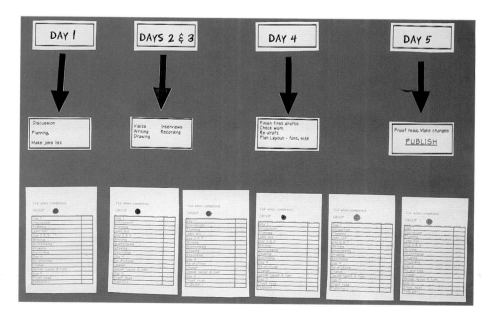

## DAY ONE

Ask each group to make the final decision about what they will write about within the topic for that page. They should consider the following: how much space is available, whether they will use photographs or drawings, who will do the writing and drawing, whether they will need to make a trip out of school, etc.

By the end of the day they should have a clear plan of the jobs they need to undertake. Ask them to make a list of the jobs with the names of the children responsible listed also. Add this information to the class notice.

## DAYS TWO AND THREE

Arrange visits and interviews, make rough notes, start drawings or paintings, take photographs, etc. Most of the work should be put on to the computer immediately, even as a rough draft. If the children choose to use a tape recorder for interviewing they may need some support to transcribe the tape. It may be best if they listen to the whole tape and then write from memory - returning to the tape only if they cannot remember it all. Word for word transcription takes too long.

Remind the children to save any work put on to the computer.

---

Last Thursday Class 5 went on a visit to minismere nature reseve we went at 8.30 and didnt get home until6 Oclockwe went on a coach.

They have Its of woden huts that you can go in to watch the birds. They are called hides thats becose they hide you from the birds we saw lots of water birds and birds thatwade in the sea

We are gonig to have some new building at our school soon we will have a new dining hall and a better car park for the teachers cars This becose there are more children in the school now. next week we have to pack up all our clasroom the buikders are coming in the holidays ibet we dont get the new clasroom

we had a picnic on the bech it was to cold to swiming we waled a long way through the tress wehad to be very quite

Our techer is plesed becose the hall wont have dinners anymore and we wont have to leave it early toout the tables.

O  capital letters

—  spellmgs

∧  word missed out

---

title

Last Thursday Class 5 went on a visit to Minismere Nature Reseve. we went at 8.30 and didn't get home until 6 o'clock.

They have lots of wooden huts that you can go in to watch the birds they are called hides. thats because they hide you from the birds. We saw lots of water birds and birds that wade in the sea.

We had a picnic on the beach. It was too cold to go swimming. We walked a long way through the trees. We had to be very quiet.

finish

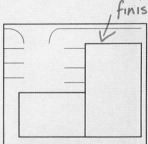

we are going to have some new building at our school soon. we will have a new dining hall, another classroom and a better car park for the teacher's cars. this is because there are more children in the school now. Next week we have to pack up all our classroom because the builders are coming in the holidays. I bet we don't get the new classroom. Our teacher is pleased because the hall will not be used for dinners anymore. we won't have to leave it early to get out the tables.

O  Capital letters

---

## DAY FOUR

This would be spent in re-drafting, finishing drawings and paintings and beginning to consider the layout of the newspaper.

Any written pieces not already typed up should be put on the computer. The children could run spell and grammar checks on their work and also ask at least one other child to read it. They should consider whether it would appear in columns, what font to use, the size of the font, what the headline will be, where any illustration will appear.

DAY FIVE

Publishing day. Each group should check through their work again. They should print off a trial copy of each page for proof reading. Give each group all of the sheets to read and to make comments upon. All the children could meet together to suggest any alterations that may need to be made. This may relate to the layout, the fonts and font sizes, accuracy, spelling, etc.

Each group can amend their work, if necessary, and then the printed pages can be printed off. If possible, each child could take home a copy of their newspaper. There may be a local magazine or newspaper that would print some of the children's work. This would make it even more realistic.

## FURTHER IDEAS USING A WORD PROCESSING APPLICATION

### • Coded messages

The children can write messages or notes using a 'normal' font, and then change the message into code using dingbats or another hieroglyphic type font.

*I have hidden some treasure in the classroom. Here is a clue. Look on the notice board.*

This can be turned into:

OR

The children may be able to decode the second message from what they know about spelling patterns, or the code with its letter equivalents can be displayed for them to work on.

### • Decorative fonts

Some fonts are particularly decorative. Single letters can be made the size of the screen.

These can be printed off for tracing, included in art work of all types, used as headings for class displays, etc.

• **Extending Vocabulary**

The thesaurus tool on some word processing applications is very useful. Survey the children's written work for commonly used words that could be varied to make the written work more interesting. Write the words on the board or a large piece of paper for a class discussion. Ask the children if they can think of other words that have the same or similar meanings that would be more appropriate to use sometimes, for example,

> said - muttered, shouted, cried, whispered
> nice - pleasant, lovely, wonderful
> went - walked, ran, travelled, skipped
> good - well-behaved, enjoyable, fun.

These can be added to the thesaurus on the computer and easily accessed by the children as they are writing.

• **Spelling Tool**

Proper nouns and other words not found in the computer spell checker can be added to the spelling dictionary in the computer. This ensures that these words are spell-checked and that the computer does not highlight them (unless they are not spelt correctly).

Roman
toga
senator
sandal
army
buildings

• **Making spelling lists**

The children can be encouraged to look through their own written work after it has been marked by the teacher and note the incorrect spellings. They can produce personal lists of words they need to learn to spell on the computer. These can be kept in a personal dictionary.

At the beginning of a new topic the teacher can generate lists of topic words to display in the class or for particular groups of pupils to use.

• **Word families**

Word families to be learnt can also be produced on the computer and the common element can be written in a different font.

This will draw the children's attention to the letter string and help their visual memories, for example:

## Stationery

A very useful function of most word processing applications is the ability to create stationery. This means that templates can be created for various uses and stored permanently in the computer. An obvious example is a letter heading. The letter heading is designed and saved. Each time you want to write a letter this document is opened and the letter written. The letter can be saved under its own title and the original letter heading is still saved in its original form.

### MENUS

There are many uses for stationery in school, either for the teacher to print off copies for all the children for work in hand, or the children can design their own stationery for a particular purpose.

For example, the school lunch menu: a template is created and each week this can be printed off to be filled with the week's menus.

Menus for special occasions could be printed and then decorated by the children.

### WEATHER CHART

A weather chart would be another use for a template. This could either be left on the computer to be filled in by the children each day, or printed off and then completed by the children with writing and drawing each day.

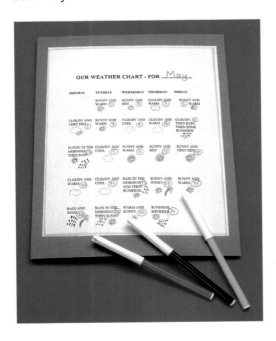

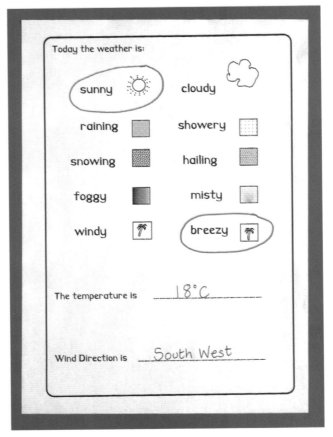

## BOOK REVIEWS

Children need support to be able to make a written response to literature. The task can be broken down, and they can be helped, by using headings under which they can record their thoughts. A template can be designed with the headings and space for their own writing.

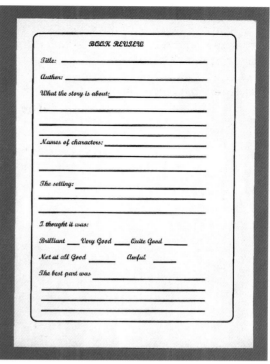

## RECORDS OF ACHIEVEMENT

These can be designed to suit the different ages of children throughout the school. The youngest children will need someone to record their thoughts and ideas, but older children will be able to complete them for themselves.

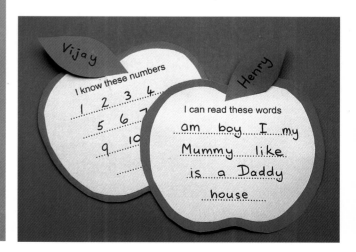

## DUTY ROSTERS

Duty rosters could be prepared on the computer and printed as required.

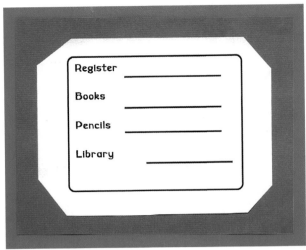

## 100 SQUARES

These can be left blank for the children to use in a variety of ways, or the children can shade them on the computer using a drawing or painting application.

## WORKSHEETS

Produce workcards by printing worksheets and mounting them on card.

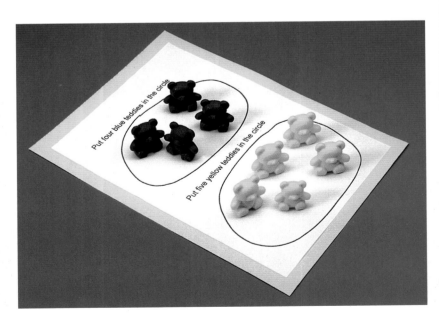

## INVITATIONS AND POSTERS
These could be for a school event and the children could fill in the personal details. The children could also design invitations for their own parties.

## READING RECORDS
The children can design their own covers for these, but the inside sheets can be made as a template to print off whenever required.

## CARTOON TEMPLATES

These could be entirely blank or they could contain blank speech bubbles. This would be useful if the children were learning about speech marks. They could write their text once they had completed the cartoon.

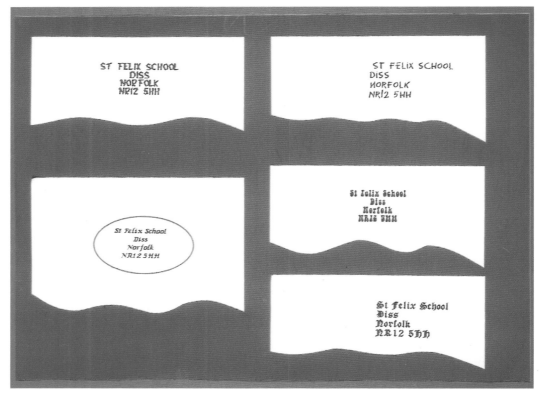

## LETTER HEADINGS

Ask the children to design a letter heading for use when they need to write letters to people outside the school.

A competition could be held for the best design.

# WORD PROCESSING PROGRAMS WITH A SPEECH FACILITY

Many word processing programs have a speech facility. This may be synthesised speech (computer generated electronic speech which sounds rather like a robot) or digitised speech (recorded human speech). Digitised speech takes far more memory than synthesised speech and this can limit the size of the stored vocabulary.

Such programs can be a powerful support for developing children's reading and writing skills. With these programs it is possible to choose whether the computer 'speaks' the text letter by letter, word by word, or in sentences. The choice will depend upon the learning objectives for each particular child.

- Introduce the 'speaking' word processors to the children by asking them to think of machines that 'speak'. Manufacturers include speech in a range of products - there are 'speaking cars' which inform drivers if one of the doors is open, the lights are on, or if the petrol is getting dangerously low. Alarm clocks have been designed that speak the wake-up calls - and there are novelty products such as talking cameras. Telephones use information technology speech for services which include the speaking clock.

- **Choose one of these products and ask the children to think of things that the machine might say.**

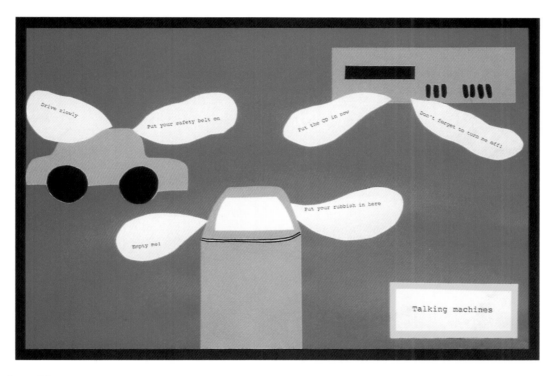

## Children's writing

- By using the speech facility the children are able to check their writing and gain greater independence. Encourage them to use the speech facility to check the spelling of words and also the sequence of their stories.
  (N.B. If the program uses synthesised speech it will say the words phonetically and will not be sensitive to the irregularities of English. For example it will say 'kat' and the child will not necessarily pick up that they have spelt the word incorrectly. This means that it is important for the children's work to be overseen by an adult.)

- Use the program to teach specific spellings. Choose appropriate spellings for individual children. Words from specific word families are very suitable as they can reinforce the children's sense of analogy and increase their ability to generalise spellings. Tell the children to look at the words very carefully. Teach them how to rehearse spellings by repeating the order of the letters. Remove the written prompts and ask the child to write the words using the word processor. When the computer 'says' the words the children are able to check if they have spelt their words correctly. As this activity requires adult supervision it is very suitable for using parent volunteers or support workers. They will need to be briefed about checking the *accuracy* of the synthesised speech.

# CONCEPT KEYBOARDS

Concept keyboards are a very useful and flexible resource. They are particularly useful for younger children or those who have limited reading or writing skills, but they can be used to develop more sophisticated learning skills or concepts. You can use pictures, symbols and words (or any combination) on the overlays and thus reduce an over-reliance on words or traditional keyboards.

- To use a concept keyboard you will need the keyboard driver, software for programming the computer (to allow it to respond when the various parts of the keyboard are touched), and a supply of paper overlays.

- The paper overlays will come with lightly drawn squares, but it is possible to make much larger cells. When introducing concept keyboards to children it is sensible not to put too much information on the overlays.

- It is important to devise a suitable storage system for the paper overlays that you create. It may be appropriate to invest in a commercially produced overlay file, as these will keep the sheets in good condition.

## Matching

- Introduce the concept keyboards with simple matching exercises. Draw pairs of pictures on the overlay. The children have to press the pictures that match. (You could use pairs of pre-prepared pictures and attach these to the overlay.)

## General Sequencing

- Develop this into a simple sequencing activity. Stick a sequence of small pictures at the top of the overlay. Use larger versions of the pictures on the rest of the overlay. The children have to refer to the sequence to press the larger pictures in the correct order. As the children become more confident, increase the challenge and ask them to cover up the sequence and try to do it from memory.

- Use the overlays for reinforcing the concept of stages of growth. The sequencing pictures could be an egg, caterpillar, pupae, butterfly; or a baby, young child, teenager, adult and an older person.

- The overlays can be used for sequencing other natural features: for example, the seasons.

- Relate the sequencing activities to everyday occurrences. **Stick pictures of a child and various articles of clothing on the overlays.** The children have to press the correct order of putting on the clothes.

| February | December | March | October |
|----------|----------|----------|---------|
| August | June | November | May |
| January | September | April | July |

- **As the children become more competent with reading and writing skills, use the overlays for sequencing the days of the week, months of the year.** They can also be used for reinforcing alphabetical order.

## Using concept keyboards for word building

Words can be broken up into *onsets* and *rimes*. *Onsets* are the initial sounds in syllables and the *rimes* are the letter strings that allow the syllable to rhyme with others. As children begin to develop their phonic knowledge, it is important that they have experience building words using onsets and rimes.

- Introduce the activity by making two cardboard cubes. On one cube write a different onset on each face of the cube, and on the other cube write different rimes. Let the children throw the cubes. They have to see if they can make a word from the onset and rime which land face up. This can be made into a game, with the children awarding themselves one point if they can make a word. Encourage the children to write down the words that they make.

- Make a concept keyboard overlay using a variety of onsets and rimes written on it. Ask the children to try and make as many different words as they can. (Note if the children approach the task systematically. Do they try all the different onsets with one rime before moving on, or do they complete the activity randomly?)

These are some suggested onsets and rimes which allow the children to generate many words.

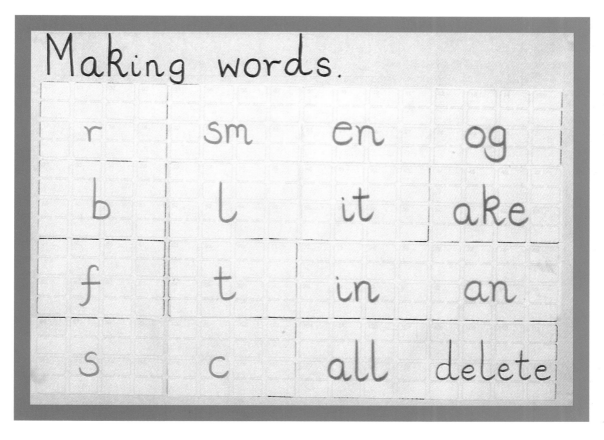

- To reinforce the letter strings, sometimes encourage the children to write down the words that they have made.

- Make collections of word families. Let the children study the families to determine which have the most members.

- When the children are confident with these letter strings, and their phonological knowledge is growing in sophistication, it is possible to develop this activity by using individual phonemes (the smallest sound units) on the overlay, and by asking the children to make different words.

- Focus on one individual phoneme. This is particularly useful for teaching the medial vowel sounds. Write the target vowel in the centre of the overlay, with other phonemes either side. Tell the children that they must make three-letter words using phonemes from the left, the middle vowel, and a phoneme from the right.

- Use the concept keyboards to teach useful phonic rules: for example, 'marker e'. Write three-letter words on the overlay and an 'e' in the centre. Instruct the children to add the 'e' to the end of the words. Ask them to notice how the pronunciation of the vowel changes when the 'e' is added. (Children are far more likely to remember rules if they have generated them.)

- Concept keyboards can be used for making words from smaller words. Choose words that include common smaller words: examples include *sometime, somewhere, something, someone, somebody, everything, everyday*, etc.

- As well as teaching children about *phonology* (the sounds within words) concept keyboards can be used to show children how *morphology* (the meaning of individual units within words) can help learn how to spell words.

- Many of the morphemic units in English have Greek or Latin roots. Tell the children about how these languages were spoken a long time ago but that you can still find bits of them in English. Children respond to the idea of a historical language detective game.

- Choose one of the morphemic units: for example, the prefix *tri-*. Tell the children that it has Latin and Greek roots and that it means 'three'. Let them think of as many words as they can beginning with *tri-*. Write these down and ask them to think about the objects and what they have in common.

- Write the prefix *tri-* on the overlay with the appropriate word endings for the children to practise making the words.

- Get the children to draw the objects to illustrate the common features.

**Using concept keyboards for developing a sight vocabulary**
Concept keyboards can support the development of children's sight vocabulary.

**Keywords**
There are relatively few words that make up a substantial percentage of all the words in text. The following 12 words account for 25% of what is written:

a      and      he      I      in      is      it      of      that      the      to      was

It is obviously important that children know these words.

Choose the words that you want to teach and write them on the overlay. Use pictures or photographs for the nouns on the overlay, but program the computer to write the word for the noun.

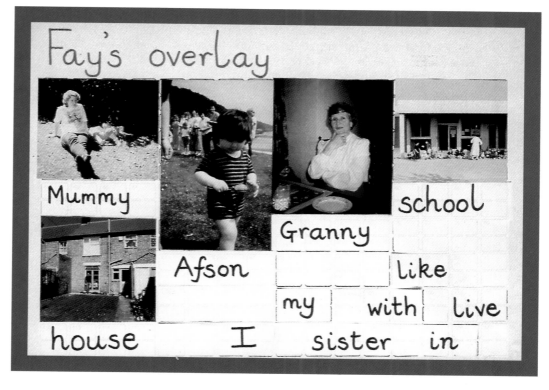

When the children have composed their sentences on the screen, print out the sentences for the children to practise reading. Let the children illustrate the sentences. The work can be made into personal 'little books' or displayed on the wall.

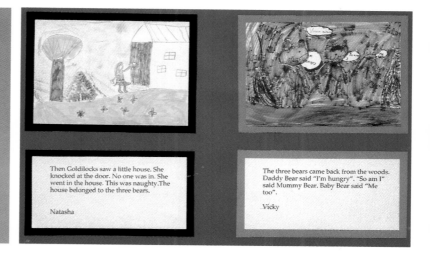

### Sight vocabulary from reading schemes

• It is important for children to know the core sight vocabulary from any reading schemes, particularly the names of central characters. Get the children to draw pictures of the characters whose names you want to teach. Write the names of the character clearly on the children's pictures and stick them on the overlay. Choose some words to include on the overlay which allow the children to construct simple sentences using the characters' names. When the children have printed out their sentences, ask them to illustrate their sentences.

The big black dog ran after the red ball

The cat ran up a tree

| up | the | ran | Sam |
|-------|------|------|-------|
| after | a | tree | dog |
| Nisha | ball | away | fast |
| red | cat | big | black |

## Vocabulary connected with specific topics

- Concept keyboards may be used to support children's writing about specific topics. They are particularly useful for those children who find writing more of a challenge. Identify the vocabulary that the children might need and write this on the overlay. The children use this as a form of topic word bank, whilst writing other words independently.

| Hermes | Acropolis | Zeus | Greek |
|--------|-----------|------|-------|
| horse | Parthenon | Trojan | messenger |
| Apollo | Aphrodite | Gods | Olympus |

## Using concept keyboards to develop story sequencing skills

- Choose a simple short story. Write the story and cut it into short chunks. Stick these on the overlay randomly. Tell the children that they have to read all the sections carefully and decide the correct order. Once they have decided on the sequence, tell them to press the sections in that order. When they have printed the story, get them to check that it makes sense.

- This activity can be simplified, for younger children or less fluent readers, by drawing simple line drawings which tell the story. When the children print off the story, read it with them.

- Use concept keyboards for the children to sequence words within sentences. This activity works best for early readers if you use sentences that the children have generated themselves. When the child has told you her sentence, which might relate to a piece of 'news', write it down on a piece of paper which the child can see. Ask the child to read the sentence back to you before you cut it up and stick it on the overlay. Tell the child that you want her to press the words in the right order to make the sentence again.

## Using the concept keyboard to introduce or reinforce aspects of punctuation

- Children can be notoriously casual about the use of punctuation! Concept keyboards are a useful tool for emphasising the use of specific punctuation marks. Write a selection of words on the overlay which will allow the children to write a number of sentences. Include the punctuation feature that you are teaching - placing it centrally to emphasise its importance. Check that the children know the rule before they start the activity.

- If you are teaching the use of capital letters, remember to include two versions of each word on the overlay, one beginning with a capital letter and the other with a lower case letter, to allow the childrren to choose the relevant form.

# GRAPHICS PROGRAMS

There are many graphics programs on the market that offer a range of options. Choose ones that provide the greatest flexibility and which the children can use with the minimum support. It is obviously a great advantage if you have access to a colour printer as this will show the children's work to best effect, but a black and white printer will do!

- Introduce the children to the various basic tools of the program. Some of these will be common to other programs (*save, print,* etc.), but others are specific to graphics programs. Many of the tools share names with objects that the children are familiar with - *line, pencil, paintbrush, shapes.*

- Once the children are aware of the basic functions, let them 'play' on the screen. As with so many programs, this is probably the best way of developing the children's confidence and competence with the facilities of the software. They will need experience of using a mouse to draw, and of rectifying mistakes they have made. When they have completed a picture, ask them to reflect on how they managed to achieve certain effects.

- Take opportunities for the children to use the graphics program to illustrate their work, or as part of the wider art curriculum.

- When the children have developed a basic competence with drawing, begin to introduce more sophisticated techniques. Demonstrate how it is possible to change the colour of their pictures without have to re-draw them. **(See photograph below, and the clown pictures on the front cover.)**

Maxine changed the colours in her picture. Which one do you like best? Maxine likes the yellow boat.

- Encourage the children to reflect on the advantages of using a graphics program as opposed to conventional drawing. These advantages include the ability to edit and change the picture until you are completely happy with the end result, and the possibility of making as many copies as you want.

- Demonstrate the possibility of multiple printings by asking the children to design a card. It could be related to a religious festival or a more general message - get well, birthday, etc. Print off the children's designs.

- This activity can be developed into a mini-enterprise. Ask the children to choose the designs that they think would sell best.

  Assign various tasks to groups of children: one group to supervise the printing, another packaging the cards, another in charge of advertising and another selling the cards.

- Ask the children to think of other ways in which they could use the graphics or word processing in their mini-enterprise. Concentrate on the ways in which they can advertise the cards. Let individual children or groups design flyers and posters for the cards. Other children can print price lists.

- Talk to the children about how many of the pictures in magazines are designed using computer graphics. Provide them with an assortment of magazines and ask them to try to identify which pictures were designed using a computer. As graphics programs are so sophisticated now, this is quite a challenge, but it can stimulate an interesting discussion. Encourage the children to describe various pictures using the appropriate vocabulary - painting, drawing, graphic, photograph, sketch, cartoon, etc.

**Exploring colour**

Computer graphics provide an excellent opportunity to explore features of colour with the children. Providing you have access to a colour monitor, the graphics program will have a colour palette which allows you to select the colour you want.

- Bring the colour palette up on the screen for the children to see. Talk about the colours that they can see. Ask them to name the colours. As there are so many colours, this activity will necessitate the children having to use other descriptive words - dark, pale and light. It will make them focus on different shades, and similarities and differences between colours. (Introduce the word 'palette'.)

- Talk about the primary colours - red, blue and yellow - and how all the other colours are made up from these.

- Provide the children with pots of paints of the primary colours. Ask them to try and make as many different colours as they can. Emphasise that they should only add a little colour at a time, otherwise everything very quickly becomes brown. Ask the children to record their colour combinations.

- Focus on dark and light shades of colours. Choose a variety of coloured paint. Tell the children that they have to add a little white at a time to the main colour. When they have mixed the colour and white paint well they are to paint a strip of the resulting colour. They then add a little more white paint and paint a strip next to the first one. They repeat this until their mixture is practically white. Display the various dark/light colour strips.

## Using prepared drawings

• Some graphics programs include pre-drawn pictures or templates. These can give confidence to children who find drawing more difficult. They allow the children to experiment with composition as they can dictate where the pictures are placed, and also the size of the different elements.

• Vary the options, with the children drawing some of the work themselves and using the custom-made drawings as well.

• If the software allows you to rotate the templates, it can be used to explore rotation and symmetry. Talk about symmetry - how the two halves of the picture will be identical. Ask the children to create a picture that is symmetrical using the templates. When they have printed the pictures, get them to draw the line of symmetry on their pictures.

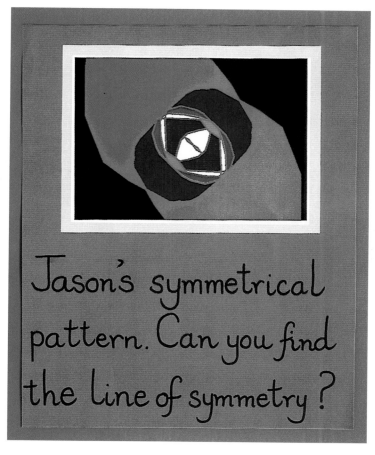

Jason's symmetrical pattern. Can you find the line of symmetry?

• With the rotational facilities on the software, the children can use the templates to create left-right sequence patterns. Encourage them to use such patterns as decorative borders on their work.

**Pattern work**

- Graphics programs give infinite opportunities for the children to create patterns. Introduce vocabulary that the children will need in order to talk about their patterns - regular, random, abstract, diagonal, horizontal, etc. The breadth of this vocabulary will depend upon the children's age and development.

- Encourage the children to look at patterns around them. Take them on a short walk around the school or ask them to look carefully in the classroom and notice any patterns that they can see. These could be part of the interior of the building (for example, floor tiles); or the exterior (for example, brick work); or the design on water covers, roof tiles, etc. Remember to get the children to look at their own clothing to observe the patterns on materials. Provide them with paper to sketch the patterns.

- Make a display of the children's sketches.

- Show the children examples of abstract art which uses pattern. Good examples include work by Jackson Pollock, Mondrian, Klee, Miro, Kadinsky, Jasper Johns and Josef Albers.

- Talk to the children about the various facilities on your graphics program for creating patterns. These might include the capacity to create random geometric patterns, using regular shapes, expanding and replicating certain designs, etc.

- Let the children experiment with specific features. It is advisable to limit the children's choice to start with as this will allow them to really explore what each facility can do, without flitting from one to another.

- Gather together examples of the children's art. Show these to the whole class and encourage them to talk about them. See if they remind the children of the work of any of the recognised abstract artists.

- Some of the work will create a sensation of different textures. Develop this by collecting samples of different types of materials, cloth and paper. Use the materials to stimulate discussion about textures, emphasising the vocabulary - rough, smooth, silky, velvety, corrugated, etc.

- Ask the children to make a collage pattern using the different materials.

- Some graphics programs can create optical illusions or distort drawings in interesting ways. Show children examples of Cubist artists. (Notable examples are Picasso and Braque.) Draw the children's attention to how the artists shatter the images and how one has to look very carefully to see the constituent elements of the composition.

- Let the children use the software to create their own Cubist art.

**Having fun with graphics programs!**
Many of the current graphics programs designed for use with children have particular features which are great fun to experiment with. It is not possible to describe all those available, but they should be described in the software manuals. Two features are detailed below.

- Joining dot-to-dot pictures is a popular activity for children. Some software allows the children to draw the dot-to-dot pictures for others to complete. This requires some skill and it is advisable to allow the children to plan their picture carefully before they embark on drawing it on the screen. Highlight that they should choose a picture which can be drawn, as far as possible, with one continuous line. They should also draw the picture quite large, as this will give sufficient space between the numbers. When the children have drafted their picture, let them try it out, printing their picture and joining the dots. Ask them if they think that they need to add any features which will make their picture recognisable. Make a collection of the children's dot-to-dot pictures.

- A function that has similarities with the number dot-to-dot lines are ones that draw with a line of letters. The standard format prints the letters in alphabetical order - so it is very useful for reinforcing the alphabet with certain children.

It is, however, possible for the children to compose their own short sentence to put into their 'word picture'. Talk to the children about what would be a suitable sentence and, once they have composed it, how they could present it on the screen. Encourage them to think about presenting it in a way that reinforces the meaning.

When they have written their sentence on the screen, let them add more graphics or print it off to add their own drawings.

Jon's dot to dot.

Morag used 'stamps' in her picture.

Brian's story in a picture.

Look at the fun we can have with our computer!

45

### Integrating text and graphics

• As children write, encourage them to think of ways in which they can illustrate their work using a graphics program. (This may require the children to manipulate two programs, and consequently to need slightly more sophisticated technology skills. When you feel that the children have the appropriate technology skills, show them how to use the programs. Write down the instructions for the children to refer to as they do their work.)

• For reluctant or less skilled writers, presenting a screen with a large illustration can encourage them to write - it is far less daunting than a blank screen.

• Some schools now have access to scanners. These allow you to scan pictures or photographs into the children's work. These are particularly useful when children are writing about school trips or excursions when you (or the children) have taken photographs.

• It is possible for photographs to be developed on CD-ROMs at many photographic developers. These can be powerful motivators for creative or descriptive writing.

### Animation programs

Certain programs allow children to animate their pictures, others are designed specifically for animation. Children find them highly motivating and they are useful for inspiring creative writing.

• Discuss different types of animation with the children. Show them examples of different forms. Ask the children how they think that the films were made. Choose some examples from the pre-computer age. This will allow you to tell the children about the length of time each shot took and the numbers of people involved.

• When introducing an animation program, demonstrate the basic functions and then let the children 'play' with the various facilities to see the possibilities that the program brings.

• Organise the children into groups. Ask them to decide on the basic story structure. Let them record the outline of their story using either a flow chart or a simple story board. The group then divides into smaller groups with each sub-group taking responsibility for an element of the story. It is better if the children complete the elements in chronological order, as this will increase the internal consistency of the resulting piece. (**N.B.** Remind the children to keep saving their work as they record their element of the story.)

The sub-groups have to plan their element in much greater detail. Check that they consider where the characters are positioned, how they move and what they might say.

**If you feel that the children require more opportunities to map out their story, tell them to make paper models of their characters and put them on long sticks (made from rolled paper).** This allows the children to move the characters and to rehearse their story before committing it to the computer memory.

- Show the whole class each group's animation. Talk about how new films are reviewed. Get the children to review each other's work. Emphasise that this should be constructive and, whenever possible, positive criticism. Discuss with the children possible words or phrases that could be used in their critiques.

- When the children have completed their animation, ask them to think how they would advertise their story and how they would summarise the plot if they were trying to sell it as a video. Show them examples of commercially produced videos as a stimulus.

- Extend this work by asking the children to design posters advertising their films. It is sometimes possible to use the animation program to take a 'still frame' from the story to incorporate in the poster.

## SPREADSHEETS

A spreadsheet can be used to help children gather, sort, organise, process, analyse and present information. There are many available to use with children.

The simplest introduction is to conduct a class or group survey about a familiar topic. The children will be able to produce a graph as a result of their work. To ensure they understand the concept of a graph and its representational nature, it is a good idea to undertake some initial work before using the computer.

- Collect a variety of objects that can be made into a three-dimensional histogram, for example, cotton reels, small bricks, match boxes, etc. Whatever is collected must be of an identical size.

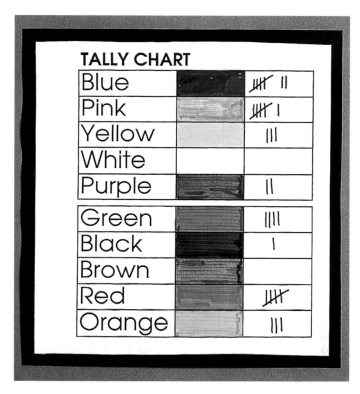

- Make a list of all the colours the children commonly use. They could look in their pencil boxes for the colours they have. Ask the children to list all the colours on a piece of paper. They should then ask each member of the class what their favourite colour is. Show them how to make a tally.

- Once they have collected all the information, ask the children to make a three-dimensional histogram of their results. The objects that are used could be covered in paper and coloured in the appropriate colours.

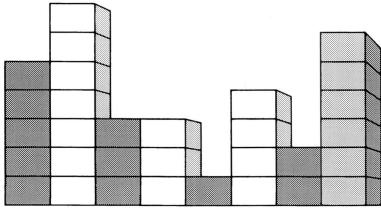

47

The children can write a few sentences about their results.

# Blue is the favourite colour.
# No-one chose white or brown.

The children can use the same information to start using a spreadsheet on the computer. Set up a template, using three columns across the page and ten columns down the page. List the colours on the left-hand side of the template and show the colours in the middle column. Ask the children to enter the numbers in the right-hand column.

The spreadsheet program can be instructed to make a simple chart of the children's results. If a colour printer is not available the children can colour the graph once it is printed.

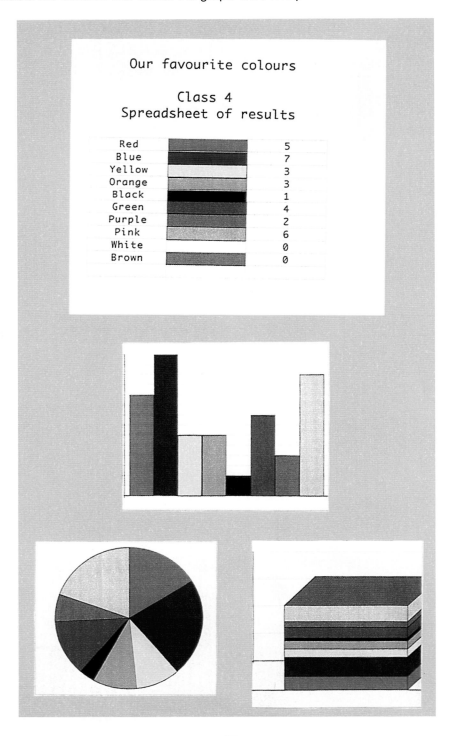

Ask the children to undertake the same survey in another class in the school. They should use the same list of colours. They can be shown that by altering the values they enter into the spreadsheet, the chart will automatically change to show the new information.

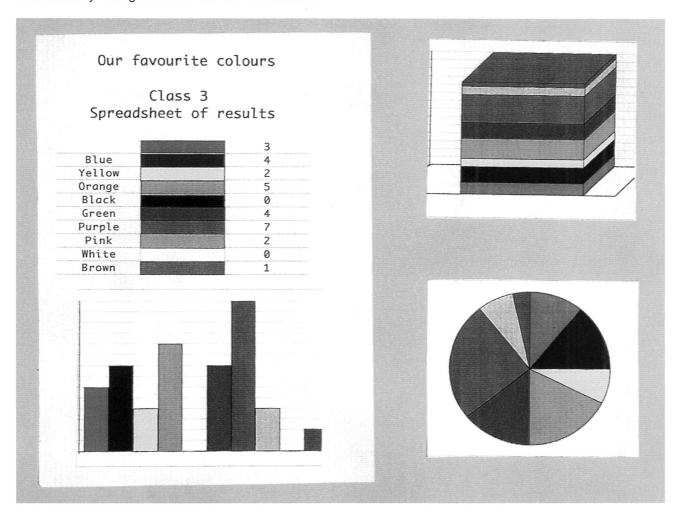

Our favourite colours

Class 3
Spreadsheet of results

| | |
|---|---|
| | 3 |
| Blue | 4 |
| Yellow | 2 |
| Orange | 5 |
| Black | 0 |
| Green | 4 |
| Purple | 7 |
| Pink | 2 |
| White | 0 |
| Brown | 1 |

Other surveys that could be undertaken to use with a spreadsheet:

- How all the children come to school, for example, school bus, walk, car, bike, taxi

- Pets owned by children in the class

- Favourite food

- Favourite playground games.

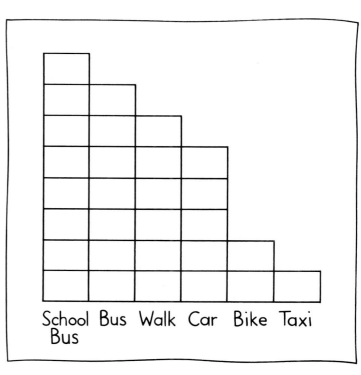

School Bus   Bus   Walk   Car   Bike   Taxi

## INTRODUCING A DATABASE

A database is like a folder in which you can file related information. The class register is a database. So, each entry is called a record and each piece of information about the child is stored in a field, for example, name, date of birth, address, etc. Other examples of database documents include a telephone directory, a library catalogue, a collection of recipes, etc. A computer can store this information electronically and make access to the information very easy and efficient.

As an initial introduction, make a collection of printed databases for the children to examine and discuss. They should think about the type of information that is being presented and how it has been categorised. So, for a recipe book, it might be: title of dish, ingredients, method, cooking time, serving suggestion. The class register might be: name of pupil, date of birth, address.

Once the children have understood the basic concept, they can make a database about themselves. Discuss with the class what type of information they could collect and how it might be categorised. Write all their suggestions on the blackboard or a large piece of paper.

Five or six categories of information are probably sufficient, so ask the children to select which ones they are going to work with.

It is helpful to include some numerical information (for example, height or weight), and a date (for example, date of birth or date started at school), etc. This is because there are different ways of presenting and ordering this information which it is useful to be able to demonstrate to the children.

Once this has been decided, define the fields using a database application and print off blank records for each pupil.

Name.............................................................

Date of Birth................................................

Travel to School .........................................

Height..........................................................

Favourite Colour .........................................

Hair Colour ..................................................

Some of the information will need to be gathered actively by the children and can be included in other lessons, for example, weighing each other, measuring each other, completing questionnaires, etc.

Arrange for the children to record their information on the computer in the database.

Show the children how they can sort, re-arrange and find information they might want. Questions can be devised that will provide the children with an opportunity for searching for particular information. For example, Who is the tallest person in the class? How many children in the class have birthdays between September and December? How many children in the class walk to school?

The entries can be printed off and the children can mount the information along with a self-portrait for display.

| Name: | Daisy John |
| Date of Birth: | 23 April 86 |
| Travel to School: | Walking |
| Height: | 1m 23cm |
| Favourite Colour: | Blue |
| Hair Colour: | Blonde |

**Further Activities**
- Using the personal information gathered, the children could make their own passports.

- Set more complex questions for the children. For example: How many children who walk to school have brown hair? How many children who have birthdays in March also travel to school by bus?

- Extend the database to other classes in the school. This would provide sufficient data to get numerical information. For example: What percentage of pupils have blond hair?

- Use a database application to record information about other topics the children undertake: for example, information about birds, plants or animals, about the local environment, historical figures, etc.

- Catalogue the class or school library.

## COMMUNICATING WITH OTHERS
One of the most potent applications of information technology is communication.

- Talk to the children about communication - ways in which people can get their thoughts or messages to others.

- Brainstorm how people can communicate with each other when they are in the same room - talking, writing, etc.

- Include non-verbal forms of communication. Talk about how you can convey meaning without saying anything. Use drama and role play to explore aspects of non-verbal communication. For example, 'How do you know someone is happy/sad/angry without their saying anything?'

- **Use simple line drawings of different facial expressions as a stimulus for discussion about other people's feelings.**

- Discuss how people with a hearing or visual impairment communicate with others. (If possible, get examples of braille and signing dictionaries for the children to see.)

- Extend the discussion by talking about how people can communicate when they are at some distance from each other. Generate a list of these forms of communication with the children. Take each method of communication in turn and talk about the part that information technology plays in each one.

- Develop a historical perspective of communication with the children. Choose a period of history before technology became current. (The choice of which historical age may be determined by linking it to other topic work.)

- Let the children try to imagine how people communicated long distance when there were no telephones, faxes, petrol-driven vehicles, etc.

  Consider the time it took for the communication, how likely it was to reach the recipient, the cost, etc.

- Create a grid to record the comparisons.

Sending a letter to Newcastle from London.....

| 1896 | 1996 |
|---|---|
| * cost - | * cost - 26p |
| * time - | * time - 1 day |
| * method - | * method - van - train - van - postman |

### Electronic penfriends
Many schools establish links with other schools and the children become penfriends. It is now possible to link with other schools using electronic mail. This can serve many purposes, not just a speedier way of sending penfriend letters between two established link schools. Children can see the advantages of obtaining information quickly from within one country or across the world.

It is useful if the school builds up contact with schools across the country or abroad who are willing to co-operate with information sharing.

This approach fits well with many aspects of topic work. In any topic where the children are required to make comparisons between two areas within a country, or further afield, they can contact a school (or a suitable organisation) to interrogate them.

- A good example would be a weather topic. Get the children to observe the weather conditions every day. Ask them if they think that the weather would be the same at different distances from the school and how they would find out if their predictions were accurate. Discuss various approaches - newspaper forecasts and reports, television weather news, etc. Stress that it would be useful to find out what the weather was like now. See if the children can suggest ways by which this could be achieved.

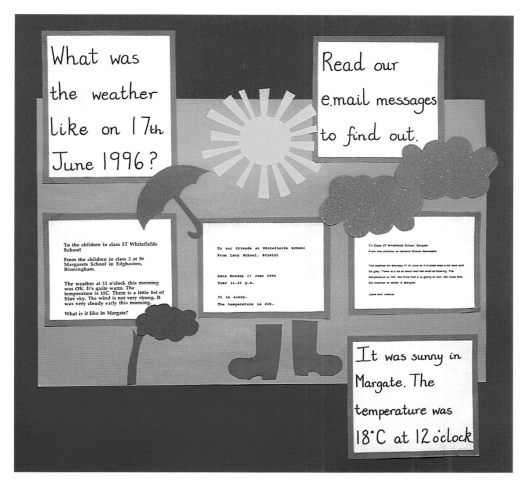

Once you have determined that electronic mail could be used, ask a group of children to compose a letter asking for the information that they require. Demonstrate to the children how to send the letter.

Ask the children how they are going to record the information as they receive it.

- Use electronic mail to discover about schools in different countries. Talk with the children about what they would like to find out: for example, the times of the school day, the timetable, the number of pupils in the class, etc. Ask the children to devise a common form on which the other schools can write down the information.

- When all the information has been returned, talk about it with the children. Encourage them to notice similarities and differences.

- This activity is very good for raising the children's awareness of other countries. Talk about the languages that children speak in different countries. Show the children examples of these languages on the replies.

- Draw on the children's experiences, as some of them might have visited the countries, to develop the work. This can be used as a springboard for investigating other aspects of life in these countries - the currency, food, weather, etc. If the children want to discover other specific facts about the countries, use the electronic mail!

- Display the information that the children have gleaned, linking it to a map of the countries that you have investigated.

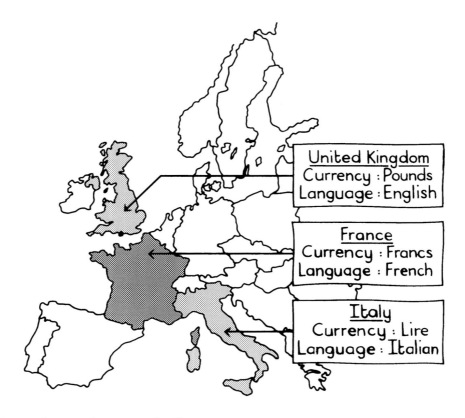

**United Kingdom**
Currency : Pounds
Language : English

**France**
Currency : Francs
Language : French

**Italy**
Currency : Lire
Language : Italian

**Comparing different forms of communication**
- Let the children think of all the ways in which they can communicate with people in different countries. Write down the children's suggestions. Ask them to consider what might be the advantages and disadvantages of the different methods of communication; these might include the cost, the speed, the reliability and how much you can send.

- Test out the hypotheses with the children. Choose a destination. Assign one form of communication to small groups of children and ask them to send a message. They have to find out certain facts about the communication.

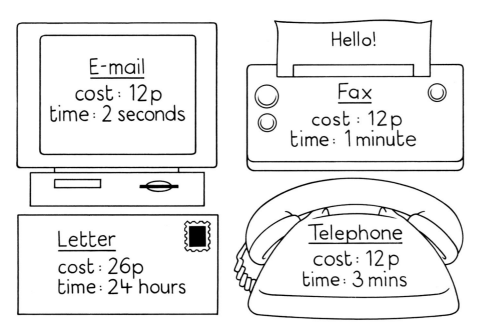

**E-mail**
cost : 12p
time : 2 seconds

Hello!

**Fax**
cost : 12p
time : 1 minute

**Letter**
cost : 26p
time : 24 hours

**Telephone**
cost : 12p
time : 3 mins

- Once the children have obtained the information let them compare the results.

- With this information, ask them what kinds of communication they and their families use. Ask them to consider who might use different forms of communication and why.

- Get the children to write what they have discovered about the communication methods. **Display their writing on relevant shapes - a telephone, a letter, a fax machine, a computer, etc., as shown.**

## MULTI-MEDIA

### CD-ROMs

CD-ROMs are capable of storing an incredible amount of data. This data can be in the form of sound, text and pictures (including video). They are a powerful resource for learning in all classrooms.

There is a wide range of CD-ROMs. Some are reference sources, others are for recreation and others are interactive stories.

As with all aspects of information technology, it is important that the children become as confident and independent in using the resources as possible.

• Introduce the CDs to small groups of children. Make sure that they can all see the computer and the CD. Stress the importance of caring for the CDs - holding the CD correctly and keeping them in their boxes. (There is a myth that CDs are indestructible - they are not!)

• Go through the sequence of loading and unloading the CD in the computer. Let each child practise the procedure.

• Get the children to write the sequence and illustrate it for display near the computer.

• Vary the ways of presenting the information - use a flow diagram or a cartoon format.

Turn on the CD-ROM
↓
Put the CD in
↓
Click on the CD icon
↓
Choose what you want to do with the CD

### Using CD-ROMs as reference sources

When exploring any topic it is important to discover whether, as well as reference books, there are any appropriate CD-ROMs which are relevant. CD-ROMs can be stored as part of the school's library resource. Make a list of the CD-ROMs and display it in the library area.

• Make worksheets to encourage the children to discover specific information from a CD-ROM.

• Use CD-ROMs which focus on artworks as a source of inspiration for the children's own art, as well as introducing them to the styles and work of great artists.

### Stories on CD-ROMs

With the addition of movement and sound, stories can be highly attractive and motivating. They are an excellent resource, particularly for any reluctant readers. They allow children to reinforce their sight vocabulary, enhance the children's understanding of the story and the sequencing of events.

### Interactive Stories

These are stories on CD-ROM which let the child interact with events in the story, usually by clicking on parts of the screen to make something happen. These events develop the story, adding a different dimension, and they are usually great fun.

When using an interactive story it is important that the teacher determines what he wishes the outcome for the child to be. Children will naturally choose to 'play' with the screen, which has value - but sometimes it is necessary to structure the activity to allow the child to maximise the learning.

- Cause and effect. Prepare a simple worksheet for the children to use on a specific page from the interactive CD-ROM story. Draw some of the characters or objects on the page. **The children draw or write what happens when they click on that object.**

- Extend this by asking the children to choose and draw a scene from a favourite story. Tell them to include as much detail in the picture as possible. When they have completed their picture, ask them to imagine that it is a screen from a CD-ROM. Talk to the child about what could happen if you clicked on certain details in their pictures. **The children write down their ideas and these are displayed around the picture.**

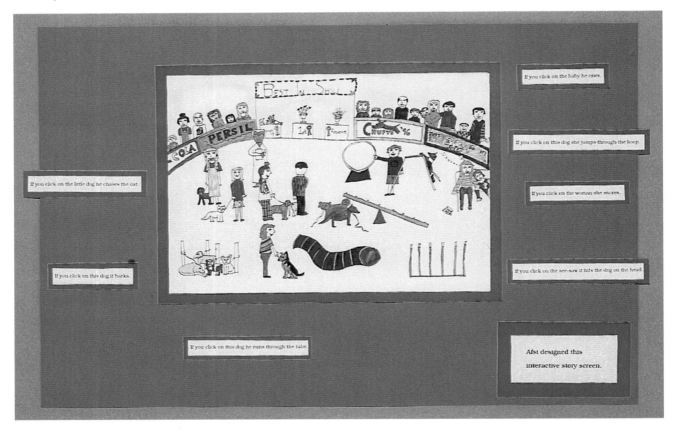

- Use the interactive stories as a stimulus for creative writing.

- Make your own multi-media stories with the children. You will need to use a graphics and word processing program and a computer which can record sound. Let the children work in small groups. Each group determines a simple story line. It could be based on a school trip or event, for example, or an imaginative story. Talk to the children about which parts of the story would be best illustrated, and the type of sounds that they could add - either reading what they have written or adding specific sound effects. The group assigns specific tasks to different group members. The tasks involved are - composing the story, word processing, recording the sound and drawing the pictures. Check that those assigned the tasks understand the procedures involved. (You may wish to write simple instruction sheets for the children to follow.)

Check that the children keep saving their work as they proceed.

# CHILDREN WITH SPECIAL EDUCATIONAL NEEDS

**Using a symbols program to write a recipe (see following page)**

Information technology is a particular benefit for children with a range of special educational needs. Computers can provide children who have learning difficulties with a non-threatening learning environment where they can experience success at their own pace and level. They can also provide important opportunities for reinforcement and rehearsal. The instant feedback available with many programs is also very important.

- There are specific aspects of information technology which can support the learning of children with sensory or physical impairments. Children with poor motor co-ordination may be able to record their work using information technology. Some children may require specific adaptations to computers or word processors: for example, children with a physical tremor may need a keyguard to help them find the correct key; others may need to use a concept keyboard. It is possible to enhance the sound output from computers for children with hearing difficulties. Children with a visual impairment can magnify the size of the print of their work or use special resources, for example, a braille keyboard, word-processing with speech facilities, and CD-ROMs with audio output to use as information sources.

- Children with specific learning difficulties (for example, dyslexia) find information technology very supportive. Specific programs may develop literacy skills. Carefully chosen word-processing activities can support their written work. In the earlier stages of their writing development, concept keyboards reduce the difficulties of the process. Word processing programs which include speech facilities allow the children to check their own work and also make spell-checkers accessible.

**Programs which use symbols**
A very useful program is one that incorporates symbols. Symbols are pictorial representations and a powerful support to all children's learning - not only those children who have special educational needs. They provide an important step for children developing formal literacy skills. There are considerable advantages using a symbols program as it reduces the burden, on the teacher, of drawing the individual symbols. Every time a particular word is typed the program matches the word to symbol and this will be displayed on the screen. It will also be printed out, if so required. **(See photograph above.)**

- Use the symbols program when you are writing worksheets for children to complete. Children at an early stage of reading development will be able to complete these without having to rely on adult support. Use symbols for writing out instructions for games or simple tasks. A good example is writing simple recipes for the children to follow (see photograph on previous page).

- Label classroom displays with the symbols.

- Create simple appropriate notices for the classroom and the school environment using symbols.

- Let the children dictate simple stories to you. Write them down using the symbols program. The children will be able to read their own stories. **Make the stories into little books for the children to illustrate.**

- Use the symbols program for making simple Records of Achievement for the children to complete.

- Children who have poor writing skills respond well to symbols used in conjunction with concept keyboards. Determine an appropriate vocabulary to use on the overlay. This may relate to specific vocabulary that you are aiming to teach the child and/or vocabulary connected with a topic. The children can use this to compose their own writing.

| I | banana | | the |
|---|---|---|---|
| | | apple | |
| strawberry | | | like |
| | don't like | | |

- As the children learn to write and read individual words, remove the symbol support from those words. Record the words that the children have learnt.

- Use the concept keyboards and the symbols program to develop the children's sensitivity to word patterns. Use symbols that belong to specific word families: for example, man, pan, van, can, fan, or cat, bat, hat, fat, etc. Ask the children to group all the words that rhyme. Encourage the children to look at the spelling patterns of the words in each family.

- Use the symbols program with specific reading schemes. Type out the text from early books in the scheme. Use the symbol-supported text with children who are encountering difficulty in developing early reading skills - let them read this text before reading the book.

- Develop symbol worksheets connected with the reading scheme to reinforce the children's knowledge.

# EXAMPLE OF TOPIC

## using word processing, database, spreadsheet and painting applications

This work is best undertaken in the winter when birds have difficulty in finding enough food. The children can help them to survive the winter by feeding them every day. The topic will provide many opportunities for observation and recording using at least four computer applications - word processing, database, spreadsheet and painting.

### Setting up a bird table
The food is best put on a bird table in a quiet corner of the school grounds but where there is an overlooking window for the children to undertake their observations. If possible, it should be sited fairly near to a hedge or tree so the birds feel more secure.

The table can be made from a plank of wood about 60cm long and 30cm wide. It should be fixed to a post at least 150cm high - so cats cannot jump on to it. The post should also be thin enough or smooth enough to prevent cats from climbing on to the table.

All kinds of scraps can be put out on the table. Bacon rind, cooked potato, fat, cheese, bread, cake, crushed biscuit, apple cores, dried fruit. Peanuts can be hung in a bag - but not salted peanuts, which are bad for birds.

It is also possible to make a 'bird pudding' which the birds love. This can be made from: fat, scraps, cereal, seeds, etc. It can be made in half a coconut shell and hung from the table - after the birds have eaten the coconut. It is possible to buy special wild bird food that contains many different seeds that may attract new birds to the bird table.

Once the table is set up, put food out every day. It may take some time for the birds to feed at it but there will soon be regular visitors. It is very important to continue to feed the birds all through the winter as they come to depend on the food put out for them.

It is also a good idea to put fresh water out each day - especially if the ground is frozen.

Have a good collection of books on identifying birds available for the children to use. Ask the children to tell you which birds they could already identify and anything they may know about bird behaviour.

**Discussion Points**
Colour, differences between male and female, size, feeding habits, nesting, eggs, habitat, migration, flight patterns, song, etc.

**Observation**
The children are going to observe the birds at the bird table each day, so they will need to consider what sort of information they might collect and how they will record the information.

It would be best if groups of children could observe informally for various periods (for about a week) before they designed an observation sheet. This would help them to think of the types of information they might be able to collect, and how to record it. Within each group, different children could be responsible for collecting different information.

Possible suggestions: overall numbers of birds, different types of birds, size and colour of birds, types of food eaten, which prefer to hang on the nuts, or feed from the table or on the ground, etc.

| <u>Colours</u> | <u>Food</u> | <u>Feeding</u> |
|---|---|---|
| Robin - Red and Brown | Robin - Bread, seeds | Robin - Table |
| Blackbird - Black | Sparrow - Bread | Sparrow - Table |
| Sparrows - Brown | Blackbird - Bacon, fat | Blackbird - On ground |
| | | Blue tit - Hanging |

Once the birds have begun feeding regularly at the bird table, organise a group of about four children to observe the bird table at the same times each day. About half an hour, twice a day, should provide the children with plenty of data and observations. The observation sheets can be collected up and kept to the end of the observation period, or the data can be entered on to a spreadsheet each day. If there is a spreadsheet available which converts the information into a graph, it is interesting to see how each piece of data changes the graph, so a daily entry is recommended.

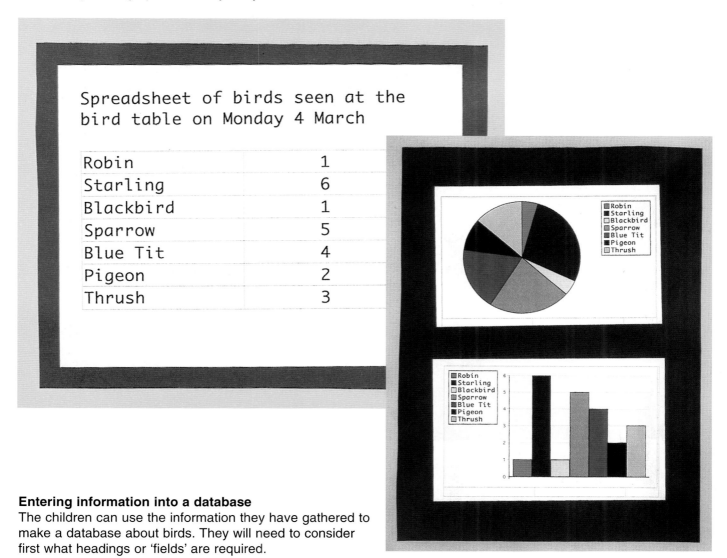

Spreadsheet of birds seen at the bird table on Monday 4 March

| Robin | 1 |
|---|---|
| Starling | 6 |
| Blackbird | 1 |
| Sparrow | 5 |
| Blue Tit | 4 |
| Pigeon | 2 |
| Thrush | 3 |

**Entering information into a database**
The children can use the information they have gathered to make a database about birds. They will need to consider first what headings or 'fields' are required.

They should look at the information they have recorded from their own observations and sort it into categories. They can also use any reference books for further information about the birds they have been observing. They can find out how many eggs a particular bird usually lays, what colour they are, how the nests are made, etc.

Using the database, define the fields that will eventually be filled in for each bird, for example:

Name:
Colour:
Size;
Food:
Eggs:

Each group of pupils could be asked to research one bird and enter the information into the data base.

This information can be printed as a list, or it can be ordered or sorted in different ways to display certain information together - for example, all the birds that lay green eggs, or all the birds under 20cm, etc.

## BIRDS SEEN AT THE BIRD TABLE

Bird      Robin
Colour    Red and brown
Size      14cm
Food      Insects, small seeds

Bird      Starling
Colour    Black, purple and green
Size      21cm
Food      Insects

Bird      Sparrow
Colour    Brown, white, grey
Size      14cm
Food      Insects, seeds, bread

Bird      Blackbird
Colour    Black
Size      25cm
Food      Worms, berries, insects

**Further work**

• Using a painting application, the children can make paintings of the birds they have observed. The printed database information can be used as a description for the painting. The pictures can be mounted for a class display.

• A variety of materials can be used for a collage of the bird table.

• A class book of birds can be produced using the database information, the children's drawings or paintings.

• Use a world atlas to track where birds migrate to and from each year.

• Make a nesting box for blue tits. You need: a plank of wood 15cm wide and about 12mm thick, a saw, a drill, a hammer, some nails, a strip of leather or rubber for the hinge, wood preservative.

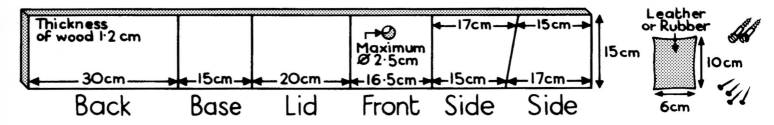

• The entrance hole should be no larger than 25mm diameter and should be approximately 50mm from the top of the front section.

• Paint the outside of the box with wood preservative.

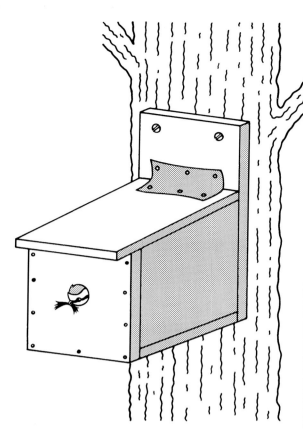

The box needs to be placed in position well before the nesting season. It should be placed at least two metres above the ground, preferably fixed to a tree, but a wall will do. It should face north and never be in the full sun.

The children can observe the nest-making, feeding the young, the young taking their first flights. The information can be added to the database.

Investigate the benefits of providing some nesting materials for the birds to use, and the need to clean the nesting box in the late autumn.

• Make a class picture showing the birds which have used the table in the school grounds, and the food they ate.

This could be displayed together with details obtained - shown as a printed spreadsheet and/or graphs (see page 61).

# INTEGRATED TOPICS
# USING INFORMATION TECHNOLOGY

## A CHILDREN'S GUIDE TO THE LOCAL AREA

Once children have become reasonably familiar with using the computer and the main applications, for example, word processing, data bases, spread sheets, drawing, etc., they can undertake more sustained work by using their skills for a larger topic.

Discuss with the children what they think children visiting their locality would want to know. You could begin the discussion by talking about their own trips to places of interest, and how they found out about events and places to visit. Ask the children to list the activities they enjoy when they are on holiday or have a day out with their friends or family.

If there are already published guide books for the area, it would be helpful to have them available.

Ask the children to think of as many places of interest and amenities in the locality as possible. List them all on a large piece of paper to pin on the wall.

Possible headings:

> Places of historic interest
> Picnic areas
> Railway station/bus stops/roads
> Play areas
> Museums
> Rural/urban walk
> Restaurants/cafes
> Library
> Swimming pool
> Leisure centres
> Cinemas
> Theatres
> Golf courses

Library                    Corn Hall
            Swimming Pool
The Saracen's Head
The Pizza Hut    The Church
Hot Dog Stall    The Mere
The Park      River Waveney

Once this information has been gathered, sort the list into general areas, for example:

> How to travel around the area
> Places to see
> Things to do
> Where to eat or stay

| Places to see | How to travel | Where to eat | Things to do |
|---|---|---|---|
| Wendy | Joe   Emma | Alex   Joy | Daniel   Kirsty |
| Michael | Christopher | John | Ben   Helen |
| Edward | Alice   Naresh | Caroline | Jane   Philip |
| Karen | David | Elizabeth | |

Divide the class into four groups and ask each group to take responsibility for one main area. If at all possible, the next step would be for each group to visit the places they intend to write about to gather information, make drawings or sketches, interview people, etc.

## How to travel around the area

This group will need access to a large scale map of the area, a smaller scale map of the region, train and bus timetables. They need to have a trip out of school to plan an interesting walk around the area. This could be an urban or rural walk that takes visitors past interesting places. The children can be asked to write a commentary on the walk accompanied by maps and pictures. When the children go on the initial trip, some of them could record their impressions on to a tape recorder and others could make sketches of buildings or plants and trees, etc.

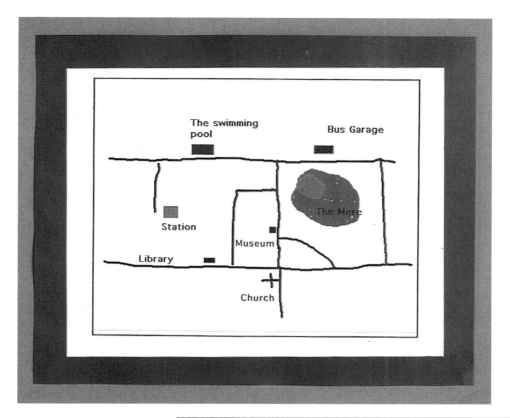

## Places to see

Ask this group to think of three or four places of interest that they think other children would enjoy, for example, a castle or other old building, a museum, shops, statues, church, a lake, river or pond. Arrange for the group to visit each of these to make notes, and to find out as much as they can about each place.

A local guide book may be a useful resource for further information.

The Mere and Visitor's Centre

## Things to do

Ask this group to think of where they go for indoor or outdoor activities, for example, the swimming pool, a local play area, a cycle track, cinema, theatre, bowling alley, etc. Arrange for the group to visit each of these places to collect further information. Many of the places will have leaflets that the children can use for information about times and events.

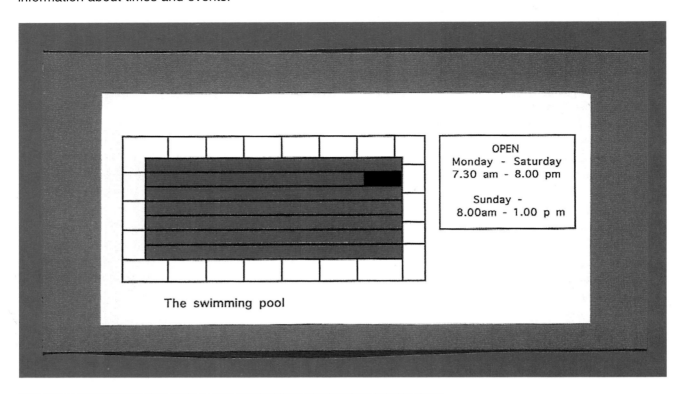

OPEN
Monday - Saturday
7.30 am - 8.00 pm

Sunday -
8.00am - 1.00 p m

The swimming pool

## Where to eat and stay

Ask the children to think of all the cafes, take-aways, restaurants, etc., they know of where they enjoy going for a meal. They could also think of places where it would be possible to have a picnic.

Arrange for them to visit some of these places to gather information about menus, prices and times of openings.

They could also investigate hotels, and bed and breakfast accommodation.

Hot Dog Stall

66

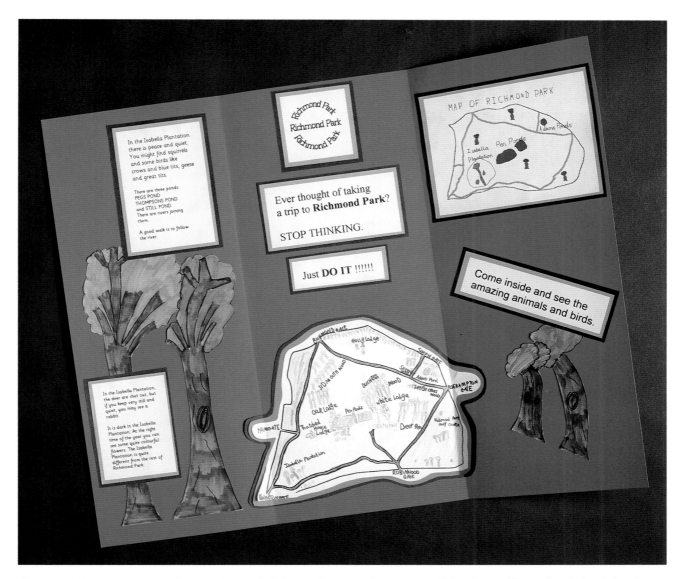

Once the children have gathered as much information together as possible, they will need to bring it back to school and decide how they will present it in the finished guide. They will probably make most use of a word processing application and a drawing application.

Each group will need to decide how many pages they want, who will write the various pieces of information, who will do the drawings and maps. Encourage them to think about the layout, the headings needed, the font to be used, the size of the print, etc.

The children should put their information straight on to the computer. The first time can be considered as a draft and the group can decide if anything needs changing or adding. It is often easier to print the first draft for the children to look at, rather than trying to look at it on the computer. In this way, each pupil can have a copy and they can make their decisions together.

If a colour printer is not available, the illustrations can be coloured by the children once they are printed.

The final guide could be placed in the local library and other venues where visitors would be likely to see it. This would provide a real audience for the children's work.

# CHOOSING APPROPRIATE SOFTWARE AND HARDWARE

As with any educational resources, it is important that one chooses appropriate computer equipment and software to develop children's information technology skills and to support other aspects of the curriculum.

There are so many programs available that it is often hard to know which to choose - particularly when the capacity of computer hardware and software is increasing at such an incredible rate.

Below are a number of pointers or things to consider when deciding what to buy:

• Programs for basic functions (for example, word-processing, data bases, spread sheets and graphics) should be as flexible as possible. These 'content-free' programs are possibly the most useful of all.

• The basic features of each program should be accessible to the children. You are aiming for the children to gain autonomy with the program as quickly as possible.

• The manual should be written in accessible language so that teachers do not have to be computer experts to understand them.

• If the programs are designed to teach a specific curriculum point, for example, a spelling rule, check that you feel comfortable with the teaching approach. Some programs can be completed 'mechanically' without the pupils understanding the concept. It is tempting to think that because something is on a computer it is interactive learning. This is not necessarily so.

• Some programs include rewards and sanctions for either successful or unsuccessful completion of tasks. Some of the sanctions are actually very attractive and children can find them motivating. This can encourage the children to 'fail' at a task, as they want to see what happens. The aim should be for error-free learning.

• Check that the program does not merely replicate something that could be done in more traditional ways.

• Remember that the software will most frequently be used in a busy classroom. If the programs use sound, will the children be able to hear it? Or, conversely, will the computer be so noisy that it will interfere with the work of other children?

• Does the software encourage desirable learning habits in children? Does it encourage self-checking, rehearsal, problem-solving, and a need for accuracy?

• Some software includes the capacity for recording pupils' responses. This can be a useful additional source of information for teachers' assessment.

• What are the children's reactions to the software? Do they respond to it well? Do they find it attractive? Do they choose to use it without being prompted? Answers to such questions can often be gained from talking to colleagues.

• Possibly the most important consideration of all: Does the program enhance the pupils' learning?

# THE INTERNET

One of the most exciting recent developments in information technology has been the establishment of the Internet (Information Super Highway or the World Wide Web). The Internet provides access to a huge range and quantity of information. Gradually more and more schools are becoming linked to the Internet. To access most of the information presented on the Internet requires a relatively high reading age, but it is still a valuable exercise to introduce children to the possibilities that it offers at an early age.

- Introduce small groups of children to the Internet by asking them to identify a subject that they are interested in. Demonstrate that by typing in the subject they can select a more specific aspect.

- Let the children 'play' on the Internet, pursuing their own particular interests and hobbies. (Monitor the children to ensure that they are not getting access to unsuitable information.)

- Devise specific worksheets for the children to discover information using the Internet.

- Use the Internet to gain information to support class topics.

- Establish a class project to design an Internet page about the class, school or local area. Ask the children to think about the kind of information that they would want to include on the page. For example, if it is about the class, the children may wish to include the number of children in the class, how many boys and girls, their ages, the name of the teacher, their timetable, etc. Assign different elements of the task to small groups of children - finding out the information, recording the data, etc. Use a graphics program for some children to illustrate the page.

> Class 2
> Heathfield School
> Number in Class - 30
> (Boys 16, girls 14)
> Ages - 9-10
> Teacher - Mr. Smith

- Sometimes use the Internet page structure as a format by which children can record information about topics. Ask individual children or groups of children to collate information about specific aspects of the topic. Decide on a common format for recording the information which the children follow. Encourage the children to use different programs depending on the nature of the project to record the information: for example, data bases, spread sheets, graphics programs and word processing.

  For example, if the class is doing a project about another country, groups of children could create pages on:
  - facts and figures about the country (population, etc.)
  - the weather
  - the industries
  - the agriculture
  - the religions
  - the food

- Save the children's work electronically. Run off a hard copy and make it into a topic book which the children may refer to.

**NOTES**